P9-CLB-287

Additional Endorsements for Love Heals

"Written with warmth, directness – and often, a touch of humor – **Love Heals** offers an inside understanding of spiritual healing. With courage and boldness to go past the superficial appearance of things, author Shannon Peck dives deep into the heart of the power of love to heal and offers practical advice and loving support on nearly every page!

> **Rev. Wendy Craig-Purcell**
> Founding Minister
> The Church of Today – Unity,
> San Diego, California

"Shannon Peck, a truly genuine spiritual healer, has gifted us all with a beautiful book on the power of love to heal."

> **Mansukh Patel, Ph.D.**
> Co-Author, *The Flame that Transforms*
> Co-Founder, Life Foundation

"It is a rare privilege to be the husband of Shannon Peck and have the opportunity to endorse this empowering book. I witness Shannon's humble authenticity and prevailing success as a Love healer every day of our lives. What a treasure for you, now, to experience this healing power from the inside-out.

> **Dr. Scott Peck**
> Co-Author, with Shannon Peck
> *The Love You Deserve* & *Liberating Your Magnificence*

Love Heals

Also by
Shannon Peck

The Love You Deserve:
A Spiritual Guide to Genuine Love
Co-authored with Dr. Scott Peck

Liberating Your Magnificence:
25 Keys to Loving & Healing Yourself
Co-authored with Dr. Scott Peck

All the Love You Could Ever Want!
6-tape Audio Course
Co-created with Dr. Scott Peck

Love Heals

How to Heal Everything With Love

Shannon Peck

LOVE HEALS:
HOW TO HEAL EVERYTHING WITH LOVE
Copyright © 2003 by Shannon Peck

Lifepath Publishing

P.O. Box 830, Solana Beach, CA 92075

All rights reserved. Printed in the United States of America. No part of this book may be reproduced or transmitted in any form or by any means, electronic or mechanical, including photocopying, recording, or by any information storage and retrieval system without written permission from the author, except for the inclusion of quotations in a review.

Cover by Robert Howard.

Printed   03   04   05   ♥   10 9 8 7 6 5 4 3 2 1

Library of Congress Control Number: 2003093463

ISBN: 0-9659976-8-5

Publishers' Cataloging-in Publication
(Provided by Quality Books, Inc.)

Peck, Shannon.
   Love Heals : how to heal everything with love / Shannon Peck. – 1st ed.
   p. cm.
   LCCN 2003093463
   ISBN 0-9659976-8-5

   1. Spiritual healing. 2. Self-realization. 3. Love. I. Title.

BL65.M4P43 2003   291.3'1
                                        QBI03-700310

**This book is dedicated
to the healer within you.**

Acknowledgements

My deepest heartfelt thanks go to my beloved husband, Scott, my Soul's hero and the only person who could have co-edited this work since he himself is a powerful healer. Without Scott's tremendous support, faith, and encouragement, this book clearly would never have come forth. Scott has also been a champion of my healing practice, causing me to flower and bloom into someone whom today I barely recognize from years ago.

Thank you to my precious daughter, Kaia, who is soulfully connected to me also as a fellow healer and whose enthusiasm for this book has been a wonderful catalyst.

A huge thank you to my dear friend, Janet Lynn, for her review of this book and helpful comments.

I am enormously grateful to my clients over all the years who have given me an opportunity to love them and practice healing.

I am deeply grateful to all those who have dedicated their lives to mind/body research. You are changing consciousness and empowering individuals with the greatest gift of all, to realize that the power of healing themselves lies within.

My eternal thanks to all healers who are doing the healing work on the planet. Whether you are professionally recognized and paid for your healing work, or if no one knows of your heartfelt prayers and meditations, I thank you. We feel your spiritual work and we are blessed immeasurably. And, finally, my eternal thanks to all healers who have passed, leaving us with their indelible mark of wisdom and healing.

Contents

Chapter 1

Love Heals

The healing power of Love is astounding.

Anyone with a commitment to the practice of a life of love and spiritual growth can heal. In fact, healing is easy.

Children, for example, are natural healers. They haven't yet read books or taken courses on the subject, yet their purity, innocence, and loving hearts naturally glide upward towards healing. They want to make things better. They have a wonderful tendency to follow Love's healing path.

When my daughter was in grade school, perhaps the first grade, I was sick in bed one day. She came over to me in such a loving way that it felt as though Love itself was visiting me. I felt the power of her heart messaging to me Love's healing presence. The upliftment acted as a quickening to a rapid healing because of her Love visit. I have experienced the natural Love healer within her many times over the years and it has grown to a full blown healing presence which she has learned to utilize on a regular basis now as an adult.

Each of us are natural messengers of Love. We can learn to tap within ourselves to hear the message of the heart that has the desire and ability to heal.

An ocean of Love

Each of us has concerns. We have problems and we are searching for answers – for comfort, help, and healing. Be assured that Love wants you to be healed.

Love wants you to know that you are pre-approved, pre-qualified, and deserving of all healings.

We are swimming in an ocean of Love right now, yet we protest, "What ocean? What love? I don't see any water. I'm not even wet!" But we are literally drenched in Love. Love is our very nature and essence. Love created us. Love is alive and well, operating as a law of blessing in our lives. We are swimming in the wide, infinite waters of Love's healing ocean every moment!

We cannot be separated from Love, ever. We can never be alone. Within your life, Love is operating at all times in your favor for your highest healing benefit.

It doesn't matter what you or your loved ones are going through at this moment. Love is with you and you are not alone. Love is guiding and directing your healing and your ability to help others. We need only open up to this vast Love resource, tune in, hold the space open, ask Love for guidance, and then sit back and listen.

Love is saying, "I want you healed. I want you blessed. Let me show you. Let me tell you how." Love intends for us to be healed. Really, to Love, there is nothing to heal. Throughout this book, you will learn to rise to this higher calibration of healing.

The answers are within

Because Love is the healer and Love is always present in each and every case, the healing we seek is already here. The healing we most desire is already within us, within Love. All the answers are within –

here and now. Our only real job is to get very good at listening, intuiting, surrendering, and living very closely to Love in all our thoughts and actions. This book will show you how to do this.

As you allow Love to guide your life in new ways, you will find yourself moving into Love's stream of healing, both for yourself and for others.

You will notice that, more and more, your life will out-picture from your ever-evolving spiritualized consciousness of Love. You will come to trust Love as a way of thinking and living and decision-making. You will experience the power of Love to heal. Things will get better for you.

Love heals *everything*

From the thousands of cases healed in my Love practice for over 20 years, I have seen the successful application of the tools offered in this book bring healing to incurable diseases, including cancer in an advanced stage. I have seen Love heal a young man in his thirties who was dying of a hemorrhaging liver, where the doctors said his liver was the equivalent of an eighty year old alcoholic and they gave him no chance of survival.

I have seen Love heal extreme crippling in a woman who had not noticed the toll many years of quiet marital abuse had taken on her. She was deemed incurable. And I have seen the many hundreds of times people have suffered from congestions, heart problems, infections, injuries, pains, aches, inflammations, swellings, as well as diseases. There is no limit to what and how Love heals us.

Love also heals all that our hearts are breaking from, including old hurts and wounds from ways we were treated, abuse, regrets, fears, dreads, burdens, guilt, anger, shame, grief, and so many other afflictions we suffer from – whether life-long habits or one-time incidents, whether hidden from us or blatantly known by us.

I have seen people in desperate situations from financial crises, family relationship crises, and health crises (acute and chronic) all healed. Some of these were quick healings. Some took months and even years.

Life lessons

We would, of course, all love a drive-by healing. However, in many healings, there are life lessons to be learned. Spiritual work which uncovers the ignorance that we suffer from brings light into these dark areas. Then we find healing.

We discover, through Love, that what we have been suffering from is something that we can change. Love stands by to tell us how to do this. We are not alone. Love is with us. We have not necessarily done anything wrong. We are merely on a learning curve.

The road to healing is the road of Love. This book is Love's book, messaging Love's healing methods. As you begin developing a spiritual healing practice for yourself, please go gently and allow yourself to learn as you develop your spiritual senses of intuition and ability to understand what Love is telling you. Love has infinite patience and so do you.

I have found that, no matter how bad something is, or how long it has been going on, or what others' opinions are, the tools in this healing book have met these needs with success. The simple process of opening to Love and asking to be guided is what brings forth healing.

Love's power is phenomenal to heal you.

Mountain-top Love

Think of yourself being placed on the mountain top of Love – placed *with* Love and placed *by* Love. You and Love are on the mountain top together, looking down on the problems in the valleys. The problems are not with you and have no part of you. You have no relationship to the problems except to see them as completely separate from you.

Love speaks and tells you, "These problems that you thought were yours are not yours. They don't define you. They can't change you. I have already defined you and created you as my own. I know who you are. You are mine. You belong to me. Problems can't change anything that I have created about you. I know who you are and these problems are not yours."

As you stay with Love on the mountain top, you continue to see more of Love's wonderful vista. Healing is taking place as you release the problems that are not part of you and no part of your vista of reality. This is what Love alignment looks like. This is the beginning of spiritual healing. You are looking out from the standpoint of Love's own Self. The one Self is the healing Self. It is you. It is us. It is divine Love's reality.

Practice this mountain-top visualization often as an immediate image of power. It is also an excellent image to hold throughout the day.

A life full of healing with Love

What's so great about spiritual healing with Love? The benefits of spiritual healing with Love are perhaps the best kept secret in the universe.

A life full of Love healing is a life of overall bliss, joy, love, power, and inspiration. That is not to say that you will be exempt from problems, but it does say that you will have tools with which you can meet those problems, offset many of them as they appear, and heal many even before they become a problem.

The dips brought on by crises and life challenges are less drastic when we use the healing tools of Love. A life of healing is a life of enormous immunization and defense as well as a life of inner stability and far less fear. How's that for value?

Through healing with Love, you are also capable of ending suffering. This is what Love does. The final destination of Love is healing.

Love dries tears and brings forth smiles, making things well. Healing with Love is the ultimate experience of love for yourself and others as well as the world. You can act with divine power and authority to do something about the world's – and your – pain and suffering.

Love is powerful and infinite

There is nothing fluffy or superficial about Love. Yet, in our society, love is often scornfully treated as dreamy, weak, girls' stuff, and silly. Love is often relegated to romance, mothers, children, and pets.

We are not taught accurately about the facts of Love. Still, everyone lives for love. Our culture thinks of love as human, emotional, confusing, something not everyone can have, and something that we covet. We think of love as mysterious. We are embarrassed as a society to discuss love, except in juvenile ways of snickering at sex or overdosing in our physical appearances, to the extent that we become confused about what real love looks and feels like. We have forgotten the power and healing presence of Love.

Yet Love is powerful and infinite. Love is divine. It is time to reclaim the value and power of Love in our lives, rise to utilize Love in healing ourselves, and live Love everywhere and all the time.

As we explore spiritual healing with Love, we will find that it is Love which alone holds up the very pillars of our lives. Love is the primary Source we need to consult for life direction, understanding, and healing.

We will be flying over the mountain ranges of Love, looking down deep into the crevices, getting the big picture of spiritual healing.

Looking deep into reality, we will allow Love's vision to bring forth healing into what appear to be problem areas. We will see how Love transforms what before seemed to be so hard core and actual. We will explore the fact that what you call "me" has everything to do with every spiritual healing in your life.

We will learn how healing means change and how to trust Love to bring forth the exact change needed, without guesswork. We will further explore the many tools Love offers us for understanding and experiencing true spiritual healing.

As we go forth together in this wide exploration, let us feel the enormity of Love's healing embrace every step of the way, knowing that Love writes this book in order to bring you the blessing of its great healing gift.

In short, this book is a divine event. You have opened this book to experience what Love has in store for your next step forward on your spiritual path. Expect massive healing throughout this book. Apply everything as you read. Be gentle with yourself in learning and in change. Use this book as a reference guide and read it many times as Love's healing messages sink into your consciousness, taking deep, lasting root.

Allow your new, higher views to make you feel new and different. Love's healing is about renewal and transformation. Allow this to occur. Trust Love like never before to heal your life. Don't be surprised by how fast or slow healing occurs, because healing is often very different than we preconceive. That's the way of spiritual healing.

Be willing to expand past your set boundaries. Allow Love to move you through areas of personal discomfort and listen for Love to guide you, allowing many healings to take place within you.

More than mere theory, this book is packed with solid healing principles and skills for your immediate use, for healing yourself, healing your loved ones, and healing the world.

Expect this book to create huge shifts in your consciousness. Everything I write about is the result of what I have learned during decades of my spiritual healing practice. As you learn to open to Love, to listen and follow Love, the divine Presence will lead all your healings and you will find the empowered life of healing with Love.

It is my deepest prayer that you have a profound, healing experience with this book. Through Love's healing power dawning in your consciousness as a result of the tools you practice in this book, Love will prepare you for an entire lifetime of spiritual healing. Love is with you on every page, in every word, and between every line.

Chapter 2

Love is Universal & All-Inclusive

Love embraces every single one of us. Regardless of what may be your background or personally held beliefs – your religion, church, tradition, family, or culture – Love is universal and all-inclusive, uniting us all.

Infinite paths, one Love

There are infinite ways of accessing and understanding Love. The number of paths to Love are limitless. This is the wide field where your life and heart need freedom to roam.

Each of us, as a Love being, is growing. We are not the same person we were even a few years ago. We have outgrown past beliefs that we once argued to be true and factual. We have learned from our experiences and mistakes. A few years from now, we may find ourselves different once again, having dropped today's most adamantly held beliefs.

In our wisdom we ask, "Who are we to judge where anyone is on the path of Love?" Do you honestly want someone judging you as you also find the way? There are infinite ways of looking at the divine. All of them are right if they are based on love for all.

All my life, my mother encouraged me to question what I believed to be true about God and take no single person's word for it. She encouraged me to explore all avenues and decide for myself. She was convinced that no one can give you an experience with God. A divine experience is between you and God alone. I have come to the conclusion that my mother was right.

It is up to each of us to reach out for our own experience. And, in that reach, it is up to each of us to allow that seed of our experience with God to grow and expand in our lives and become the leading point of all that we do.

There are no greater rewards in life than your own personal connection with the divine. Spiritual healing is based on it.

Though we may have valuable help along the way – from healers, ministers, spiritual teachers, priests, monks, family members, friends, or anyone who leads and models a spiritual life – the individual choice still lies within each of us to reach out in healing prayer for guidance and a deep, personal relationship with Love.

This is not an overnight experience. It is a constant learning, growing experience of listening for divine Love's healing direction. This is the path of spiritual healing.

If you have not had your own individual experience with divine Love, pause now and ask Love to guide you in this experience. Continue to be in this open place, ready for Love to guide you.

My personal search

I was blessed to be raised by two loving parents who modeled love, wisdom, principles, respect, and fairness. Growing up, I attended a Southern Baptist church. Yet, in grade school, I loved to practice giving communion to my Jewish best girlfriend.

By the time I was sixteen and had my driver's license, I drove myself to a Presbyterian church and joined. Several years later, I found myself studying the Catholic catechism over the summer months, often meeting with a priest to discuss what I was learning.

When I was in my twenties, I left church altogether and even left God. Nothing made sense to me. After several years of searching, I realized that I was on a spiritual path, in search for Truth.

I then studied "The Science of Creative Intelligence" taught by Maharashi Mahesh Yogi. I practiced Hatha yoga and transcendental meditation, and experienced psychotherapy, group therapy, and occasional marathon therapy weekends. Still I searched.

Closing my twenties, and continuing my quest for truth, I was introduced to Christian Science and become an ardent student. My great passion for healing led me to become a registered Christian Science practitioner for sixteen years. I also was appointed by the church to give lectures on Christian Science. It was through the study of Christian Science that I had full, mega doses of Truth and learned how Truth heals.

Though I no longer consider myself a Christian Scientist, I place the highest value on its focus on spiritual healing and I cherish all that it taught me about healing.

As my life continued to expand as the co-founder – with my husband, Scott – of TheLoveCenter, a non-profit educational organization dedicated to "holding the space for all humanity to live in healing Love," I came even more into alignment with Love as universal and all-inclusive.

I found myself speaking as a spokesperson, not for a religion, but for Love Itself. In fact, Love caused me to re-define myself as a spiritual healer-at-large, available to serve anyone in the universe in search of healing and to do so in a non-denominational way.

Love's universal and all-inclusive nature has caused me to be open and honoring of all paths to Truth.

Today I have calls for healing from people of many varied backgrounds – Buddhist, Christian, New Thought, Jewish, and people who do not embrace any religion. I work with people from any belief system who have a genuine interest in spiritual growth because spiritual healing is synonymous with spiritual growth. And I love them all!

Think about it. Does Love really see us divided by religions? Does Love look differently at a Catholic or a Muslim? Would Love stand in judgment of you? No. Love only sees its own magnificent expression in each of us. In fact, Love sees each of us as its own.

A marriage made in universal & all-inclusive heaven

When Scott and I decided to marry, we needed someone to marry us. I was a member of a ministerial council in Los Angeles and Scott asked me which of all the ministers I felt most spiritually connected to. Though I loved all the ministers, Love selected a deeply spiritual Rabbi, whom I greatly admired. He joyfully agreed to marry us. We loved his open-minded willingness to marry two non-Jews. We felt included in his wide embracing circle of love.

Even before we married, Scott and I had many discussions about not confining our love just to each other. We knew that we had an incredible relationship and it was important to both of us not to limit our love. We wanted our love to be universal, excluding no one. We wanted to be global in our love. And we are.

The infinite embrace of Love

Over and over in my healing practice, I receive calls from people who say, "I called you because I knew you would love me and you wouldn't judge me." How we long for the healing love of God!

Love is ready to heal all who honestly seek spiritual healing, regardless of their beliefs. We may grope for clarity in understanding what is truth. We may have different ways of describing what is most meaningful to us, and how we think of God. But there are infinite paths to Love and all of them are correct if they express love. Each of us is included in Love's healing embrace. And we can do this for others.

Begin now embracing everyone – regardless of labels, background, stigma, nationality, tribe, or race – as Love's own, richly deserving your love. Rise above separateness and practice unity.

The more we practice Love, the more we become like Love. Healing naturally follows.

To come into greater Love alignment, let yourself become more open minded and non-judgmental. Then you will recognize that Love is present and available to you at all times. It's a great way to double the amount of love in your life too. In fact, when you think of humanity, begin the practice of opening your heart to everyone. This is healing every time you practice it.

Think of it this way. Nothing is external to Love. Love knows no divisions. All reality takes place within Love's kingdom whether or not life presently appears this way. As far as Love is concerned, there is nothing else that exists. Love includes each one of us. The divine Us is Love. The only Self is Love. Love is all there is. Love is here now. Healings take place as we awaken to this realization of Love's Allness.

Moving our lives into the space of universal and all-inclusive Love enables us to be at one with our Highest Self, the focus of the next chapter.

Chapter 3

Your Highest Self

This may surprise you. At the core of every spiritual healing there is always one question being addressed: Who are you?

Healing begins the moment you begin to identify yourself as divine and of divine origin. This is what I call your Highest Self. The more this is explored, the more healing is experienced.

As you continue reading, I wish to make a request of you. Be prepared to throw off limitations about how you view yourself and open to seeing yourself as divine – as Love sees you. This brings forth healing.

This may be radically different from how you are accustomed to viewing yourself. Yet, without a spiritual view of yourself, there is no basis for spiritual healing.

Discover Your Highest Self

The phrase "Highest Self" describes your God Self or Love Self. Highest Self describes who you are at the highest level of Truth and reality. In Truth, you have no other self.

You might have other words for this, but the phrase Highest Self helps us to remember our true identity as divine Love.

Since your Highest Self is indispensable to spiritual healing, let's look at the different ways we could describe your Highest Self.

Consider the descriptions below and how they describe who you are and who you have always been:

- Love's Self
- Love's only "Me"
- Your core self
- Your Soul self
- The only I AM, or identity
- Your authentic self
- Your enlightened self – filled with constant healing inspiration
- Love's healing presence
- Your true essence and nature
- Your sacred self
- Your perfect being
- Who you call "Me"
- The one "I" or "Us"
- A blessing
- Blessed
- Holy
- Innocent
- Pure
- Wise
- Powerful
- Beautiful
- Loveable
- Capable
- Always at one with Love

Have you ever described yourself in such wonderful terms as this? Let's claim this description for you right now.

Review the Highest Self list with the realization that this is the Self you have always been. Pause now and spend some healing moments honoring and truly loving your Highest Self. I hope that you will come back to this page often and rehearse this all-important exercise of remembering who you are. Please feel free to expand the list by adding many more ways of describing your Highest Self. Let Love tell you. And be sure to love your Highest Self.

Love is opening up new views for you to see the vast beauty of your Highest Self. The Highest Self translates humanly into:

- I am good, not bad.
- I am loveable, not unlovable.
- I am important, essential, and of infinite value to the universe.
- I am divine.
- I am part of an infinite, divine plan operating as a blessing to all.
- I am included in all of Love.

Release your false self and walk in the Light

When thinking of your true self, please release all the thoughts that say you are wrong, guilty, hurt, old, angry, evil, ugly, worthless, condemned, doomed, unwanted, un-belonging, discouraged, afraid, and doubtful. This is not your Highest Self. To continue describing yourself in negative ways would be a great loss to yourself and to the world. It would mean the loss of your fullest expression.

The simple, daily practice and focus on loving your Highest Self will cause you to grow and become more visible in your godliness.

All the world's Highest Selves are saying, "Please come forward! We need your Highest Self! We can not offer our Light's fullest shine without you! Let your Light join ours and together we will shine as Love's full brilliance." Your Highest Self is also your healing self for others.

Great spiritual leaders embodied divine greatness. They so clearly accepted their true state of spirituality that to be in their presence was more than an uplifting, holy experience. Healing took place. Their acknowledgement of Love's power and their all-inclusive embrace of humanity uplifted thinking and left an immense imprint on civilization. They were "Highest Self" Masters. They are our models.

Your fullest magnitude

Let's discuss this further. Consider the magnitude of your life. How bright and big is your radiance? When we measure stars, for instance, we measure them by the magnitude of their brightness. Imagine for a moment what your life would be like if you lived at your fullest magnitude. What would that look like and what would be the effect on the universe?

Much like the night gives place to the beauty and power of a single star's brightness, each of us has the capacity to illumine the universe with our gifts.

We each came with Love's gifts such as nurturing, healing, envisioning, building, uniting, humor, beauty, music, joy, enthusiasm, inspiration, empowerment, communication, expressing calmness, peace, stability, and infinitely more. You can discover your gifts by observing what gives rise to your innermost passions or the best words people use to describe you. Your gifts are immeasurable, incalculable, and enormously healing. They have magnitude.

Now imagine how Love defines your magnitude. Love's view of your magnitude might be labeled Absolute Magnitude, your ultimate illumination of Love. So the real question is, "How close are you right now to shining at your Absolute Magnitude?"

It is Love's design that each of us rise to our Absolute Magnitude and fully utilize our gifts. Living out from your Highest Self is the key. No matter where you are presently in your life or how difficult your life may be, begin today living from your Highest Self.

Mentally hold this place and be willing to release all that would hold you back.

Overcoming resistance to living our Highest Self

One of the biggest ways we are held back from shining at our brightest is from our own thinking. It is our inner resistance. You might, of course, ask, "Why would anyone resist something so wonderful as realizing their full potential, their brightest bright, their Highest Self?"

Resistance is subtle. It shows up with inner talk such as, "This concept of me is too big. I'm not worthy. Who am I to have such radiance? What if I fail and disappoint people – or myself?" Resistance also shows up where your intellect argues with your heart. It complains, "I just don't understand all this!" We further resist by holding our Highest Self at bay until we see "how" we're supposed to carry it out.

Overcome such resistance by releasing the *how* and simply radiating the magnitude of Love in your caring heart. There is nothing to stop you. Begin imagining how wonderful you will feel living *at one* with your Highest Self.

Be mindful not to judge yourself as being too big or to discount yourself as unworthy or to label this as egotistical. Isn't it Love's grand nature to shine brilliantly? Isn't this our mission, too, as Love's ambassadors on earth?

Your shine is healing to yourself and to all others. Imagine your brilliance equal to a heavenly star expressing the light of Love with full-scale brightness. Imagine radiating your compassion, understanding, patience, gentleness, and caring love to such a degree that you are a healing presence to the entire universe!

It doesn't take words. You can sit at home in a chair or on the floor and practice opening your heart to the fullest and shining grand Love to all.

As you hold to the magnificence of this wonderful expression of yourself, please know that there will be times you may doubt all this to be true. You will even be sad that it seems distant or unlikely.

You will have times when you lose your faith, telling yourself this is just something your ego dreamed up so you would feel valuable. These are merely times when your old self is trying to go home and is disturbed that it cannot find its old resting place. You outgrew it. Good. That's what your healthy life looks like.

You are not lost. You are not even confused. You are still on track. Such times are a reminder for you to drop the burden of being your old self. Allow yourself to rise to your true self, qualified to be at your Absolute Magnitude of Love at all times, including now. Present your Highest Self to yourself!

We also sometimes get so involved in other people's life dramas that we abandon ourselves, identifying with them – through sympathy, curiosity, or even admiration. Where did we go? Our Highest Self has the ability to bless and carry the power of healing through our love and wisdom. What a major benefit we are to each other when we stay grounded in our true identity! It is essential for you to occupy your Highest Self and not vacate who you are.

Gently remind yourself that you are capable of navigating through life changes with wisdom, comfort, calmness, and peace, rather than through emotionalism. Sit quietly within your Highest Self. Sweetly begin to occupy your light, your brightness of love, your Absolute Magnitude. Realize your God Self.

Come out from your timidity and be all you were created to be. The universe needs your brightest love – and now. Dare to be as BIG as you truly are!

Step into your light. Your light encourages other's light. Do you feel the universe enlightening? You have been created by divine Love to represent Love on earth. This is healing.

Choose the door to healing

Healing is a divine, not a human, event. Everything in the human experience defines you as vulnerable, afraid, and certainly not divine. Yet we always have a choice. We can choose which door to open.

Door number one is the door to healing. It represents your Highest Self. Door number two is the door to suffering. It represents the belief that you are not from Love, that you are an isolated self that is alone, struggling, and entirely separate from Love. Which door do you go through for your healing? Which door best identifies who you truly are? Door number one or door number two?

One night, I woke up feeling ill with a sore throat. I was flooded with thoughts like, "Oh, no, I don't want to be sick!" and "I wonder if I got this over the weekend when we were with several hundred people all sitting close together in an auditorium?" And "Will this take a few days to heal and will I have to cancel my plans?"

Actually, when I woke up, I found that I was already, automatically, entering door number two, the door of suffering – without even asking for it! We rarely consciously choose door number two.

Within seconds, I stopped the runaway train of thoughts and reasoned from door number one – the door of healing which represents my divine and true self, or Highest Self.

The answer to *who* you are also answers *how* you are. "If I am divine, then I must be exempt from illness." I continued to identify my genuine self as divine. I made every effort to move through door number one, the door of healing.

I reasoned that I am Love's own and that Love is here abiding in me as my experience and understanding. I reclaimed my true identity as Love's offspring, under Love's healing care. Within moments, I trailed off to sleep.

When I awoke the next morning, I felt much better – though there was a trace of the sore throat still there. Again, I opened Love's door, the door to healing, and I continued to focus there. "I am divine. I live in Love. Divine Love does not have illness and neither do I."

Throughout the morning, I continued to remember and affirm Love's presence with me. Many times, I thought of myself as Love, as Love's very presence. This ongoing practice – lasting for a few moments at a time – caused me to practice my true identity as divine, my Highest Self.

By late afternoon, I was able to spend time in deeper thought. I focused on my true identity as Love's perfect self while I released symptoms that mentally suggested I was not Love's perfect self. During this time, occasional swallows caused me to feel like I had run back to door number two – the door to suffering – trying to convince me that I still had a sore throat. Yet eventually, I was able to drop these thoughts entirely and stay in my true Love Self, free of the illusion of something wrong. I experienced physical healing as well.

Who am I? The answer needs to be decisive. I conclusively decided that the question of my identity had been answered without vacillation. Love showed me. I was back in my Highest Self. I was healed. I successfully stayed in the doorway to healing.

My healed condition was determined by remembering that I was Love's Self and not someone who was suffering with a physical problem.

Packed into the focus of seeing myself *as* Love's Self came Love's healing guidance and assurance. My fears were quieted as I leaned on divine Love for all my information. These assurances from Love caused me to feel more convinced of my true divine Self because they felt so right, peaceful, and comforting. I felt the divine presence of Love's healing action that day. I walked through Love's healing door and consciously occupied my Highest Self. You can do this too.

You and Love are One

Whatever is taking place within Love right now is exactly what is also taking place within you right now. Love is peaceful, harmonious, perfect, whole, complete, caring, and beautiful at this moment, and so are you! This is the permanent condition of your Highest Self. Love made you. You are Love's expression.

Think of the sun with its rays radiating outward. Each ray is of the sun. Each ray unites with all the other rays and presents brilliant light. In unison, there is one brilliant expression of the sun. Without the rays, there would be no sunshine. Without you, Love would not have a full expression. You are a total necessity to Love.

As Love's beam of light, you emanate from Love. Love is your source of life, energy, light, intelligence, action, and purpose. Love is your identity. You exist because of Love, which created you. You have meaning and essence because of your Love origin. Everything that happens to you is a result of your identity as a Love beam of light, flowing from Love, your Source.

We have an incredible rate of forgetting this all-important truth. In fact, healing hinges on the fact of your remembering and living this fact that you are a Love beam of light and this is your true identity.

No other information about your identity need be considered by you. If, for example, information tells the sun ray that it is a star, a planet, or a meteor, this information about its identity will be disqualified because it is not the true fact.

This is exactly the work I did the morning I woke up and I contemplated thoughts describing me as someone who had a problem with a sore throat. Really?

Did I overnight stop being the child of Love? Did I overnight drop out of Love's presence and become something else other than Love? Did I even remotely lapse from Love during the night while I slept? No.

I continued to reason according to the facts describing my identity as Love's own Presence. My perseverance continued to rule out symptoms of illness, until, in the end, the one identity of myself as Love prevailed.

How much did I suffer? Hardly at all. How much would I have suffered had I allowed the sore throat to continue by not challenging it? I most likely saved myself from spending a few days in bed with illness.

Over the years, I have found that, by applying what I understand to be my divine identity rather than a view of myself as a struggling mortal, I have exempted myself from suffering from most illnesses.

You and Love can never be separated – ever

This is the best news you will ever have.

No matter what problem you presently face, and no matter how critical or drastic your need is for healing at this moment, Love is totally present with you and available to you. All of Love is being poured into your life at this and every moment as an all-caring, loving Presence.

Do you realize what this means? It means that you are not alone, not ever. It means that the solution – to whatever you think your problem is – is present and available to you now.

At this moment, Love's healing presence is the Presence that helps awaken you to remember the fact that you and Love are one and all is well.

Does this apply to your present physical problems? Yes indeed. Physical problems are not representative of your Highest Self and therefore they do not represent you, ever. Physical problems are as much an illusion as the sore throat I experienced, because our identity as Love is all that truly defines us.

If this seems vague, don't worry. We will be discussing this in greater depth throughout the book.

Looking at life from your Highest Self

Imagine the power and joy of staying centered in your Highest Self. Healing inevitably occurs when we use our Highest Self as our:

- Measuring Stick – for all reality. It is your standard for sorting out what is your real self and what is not your real self.
- Filter – for everything in your life. Whatever you are calling "me" each moment can filter through Love so "me" and "Love" are one.
- Tuning Fork – to get everything in your life in tune. A tuning fork is a device you use as a perfect pitch for tuning your instrument. You want everything in your life tuned to your Highest Self's wisdom.
- Holistic Alignment – A car needs service each 5,000 miles. Your Highest Self needs Love-service every day – to recall your identity as divine.

How often you go to your Highest Self will determine the quality, value, and healing power of your life.

When you are at one with your Highest Self, healing occurs naturally. And when you fall out of your Highest Self, you lose touch with healing.

Let me give you another example. While having a really hard day, it felt like I was moving through thick quicksand. Everything was stressful and difficult. Scott asked me if I planned to attend yoga class later that afternoon. I thought about it and decided not to. I thought I would just stay home.

At the last minute, I decided to go and use the yoga practice to address and work through the problem. It turned out to be a very good idea.

As I moved through the yoga positions, breathing deeply, I became more relaxed. As I became more relaxed, I felt more like my true self. As I felt more like my true self, I began to get in touch with those things that were bothering me.

Moving through the yoga practice, I realized that I was angry. I simultaneously decided to let it go. I realized that I was carrying the burden of worry. I also decided to drop that as well. These things are not my true self. I didn't have to fix them, just to let them go.

In fact, as each of the negative feelings appeared, I decided that it did not truly describe me and could not then pull me in to act out its drama. After all, how can a Love beam be filled with light and at the same time have dark places, too? The answer is that it cannot.

Pause now and take a nice, deep healing breath. Breathe in Love. Do this a few times. Are you beginning to remember who you are? As you awaken, allow the dark places to be filled with Love's healing light. Breathe out all that does not belong to you.

Dark places tend to carry a load of weight – burden, fear, and worry. Now breathe in more Love and, as you exhale, allow the dark weights to fall away. Dark places and dark weights do not belong to you. They do not correctly describe your life, your present situation, or your reality. Let them go. Surrender more to your beautiful Love Light. Allow healing to come in. Allow Love to meet your needs in a new way, and perhaps in many new ways.

Let's together hold the space for your wonderful Love identity to be known and fully realized by you.

Do this each day and journal what Love shows you. If you don't have time to journal, just spend Love moments throughout the day where you accept yourself, drop weights, honor your beautiful Light, and allow your Love to shine, shine, shine.

If you go to your Highest Self only when you have a problem and need something healed, your full healing potential will be limited because you will be tuned to the Light only momentarily. This is actually harder than staying in your Highest Self on a daily basis.

If you go to your Highest Self as a daily habit, however, you will be a continuous healing presence to yourself and others. You will be experiencing your spiritual healing power at the highest level. There is no way to describe the beauty, joy, peace, and power of this way of living. It is the life of a healer! It is the life you deserve! It doesn't happen overnight but, by making the daily effort, you will succeed.

Get acquainted with your Highest Self. Your Highest Self is what creates all your God moments and all your healings.

Your Highest Self is the Love Light within you which has the power to cancel all the darkness – harmful patterns and habits, toxic emotions and energies, and trouble and problems of every kind, and for all time.

Open yourself to the divine Presence greater than yourself, but of yourself. This is the Presence or Self that heals everything. This Presence is full of Love.

Go to the healing place. Your Highest Self's perfection is present, active, and real.

Rise into the Light of your Highest Self.

Staying tuned to your Highest Self opens the door to connecting with Love through intuition, our next healing focus.

Chapter 4

Connecting with Love through Intuition

Through intuition, you can connect directly with divine Love, the source of all healing.

What a great comfort to know that whenever we call on divine Love, it is right here – present and available – whether in the middle of the day or night, on land or sea or space, in joy or danger, in crowds or alone, whether we're young or old, whether we're rich or poor, whether we're healthy or unhealthy, able or disabled, blind or seeing, deaf or hearing.

There is no circumstance in which you can possibly find yourself where Love is not already there accompanying you. This is guaranteed by Love's ever present Allness.

Love is, in fact, incapable of absence from you. From Love's standpoint, you have always been with Love and Love has always been with you. This is the way it has always been and always will be, without exception.

How then can we access Love's presence?

When I was about 10 years old, my Dad called me and my brother to the living room for a meeting. This was the only time he ever did this and we knew it was important.

Once we sat down, he told us that he wanted us to remember two words for the rest of our lives and live by them. The two words are *be aware*. This made a deep impression on my brother and me. Be aware. Of what?

Dad left that to us to figure out. I have been so blessed by these two wonderful words all my life. My interpretation of his advice is to be *spiritually* aware. Be aware of Love. For example, Love's all knowing intelligence is continually unfolding messages. What is Love saying right now to you? Learning to intuit Love's healing messages brings forth healing.

Love has no desire to be mysterious or unknown. Love's desire is to be fully accessible and knowable at all times. You can have your own first-hand experience with divine Love and access Love all the time. And you can experience healing all the time, since Love is the healer. Please do not underestimate intuition. It can change your life forever.

Receptivity and openness are everything in spiritual healing

Consider yourself an empty container and, when you turn to Love for healing, expect Love to fill your container. If your container is tiny, Love will fill it. If your container is large, Love will fill that too. Let your container of receptivity and openness to Love be enormous!

You will receive from Love at the rate of your receptivity and openness to Love. It's your primary job then to remain open all the time so that Love – and not emptiness and fear – fills you. Your primary fill, of course, will not be with material things. Your rich fill will be from Love's wisdom, inspiration, and perfection which provide healing.

Problems are healed by following Love's guidance. But if you are open, listening only 5% of the time and filling your mind with negativity 95% of the time, your container will be mostly filled with what needs to be emptied. Be open and receptive to have your container filled by Love. This will bring forth intuition and healing.

All knowing through intuition

Your Highest Self has all-knowingness. By listening to your Highest Self, or intuition, you receive divine guidance.

Larry Dossey, M.D. writes about parents who had been interviewed after their children died of sudden death syndrome. Studies showed that, of the parents interviewed, 21% knew "for certain" in advance that their child was in danger. Another 22% of the parents "were worried in advance," but not certain. Yet when these parents went to their physicians, they were met with their doctors' criticism.

This represents 43% of parents who intuited that there was a problem *before* the problem even appeared. Intuition is a part of you that carries a higher view to prompt you towards healing.

Doctors, of course, cannot be faulted for not being guided by intuition. Their entire training in the medical field is physical, not intuitive, and frankly, their patients expect to receive doctors' scientific opinions and treatments while under their care.

If you have an intuition that there could be a serious problem ahead, is there something you can do to prevent the problem from occurring? Yes. This is one of the values of intuition.

When you feel uncertain about a situation, it could very well be your angels awakening you to be alert to Love's healing, protective guidance. This does not mean, however, that every time you are afraid it is intuition. Through practice, you will learn to know the difference between fear and intuition.

Intuition is your link to divine healing

Intuition is at the heart of connecting with healing Love and your Highest Self. All the information and guidance you need is already within you, messaging itself to you. Intuition is your sensing of this, even in small ways. You can practice connecting to Love as much as you want.

Intuition improves with practice. As you use it, you will come to understand it more fully and learn of its immense value and reliability. As you rely on it more and more, you will come to trust it in good times as well as times more challenging. You can learn to turn to Love's healing intuition as a first response to situations since intuition actualizes your all-knowingness. What are you intuiting? Divine Love's information and guidance for you!

Intuition is the experience of reliance on divine Love. Can you really learn to live in this way? Absolutely! I couldn't heal without it.

Intuition sometimes comes as a gut feeling, a quiet, inner voice, or a gentle urging. It is the unfailing presence of Love that wants to bless you, to guide you in the right direction, to offer you a healing attitude or vision of understanding, or a simple thought.

Some people have names for their intuition. You can call these intuitions divine thoughts, angels, divine guides, messengers, celestial luminaries, or the spiritual senses. No matter what you call your intuition, it is divine Love in some form.

Your intuition is the single most important aspect of your spirituality because it is your intelligent connection to Love's healing guidance and power. The divine Self can be fully known and actualized each day through each of us. You can access this all-important information available to you by learning the following simple process.

Ask Love – open, wait, and listen

Many times every day, I tune in and ask Love to guide me. Then I open up wide to become receptive to Love's message of guidance. My container is bottomless, waiting for Love to fill it. In all my years of spiritual healing, I have found that, with every request, I receive an answer.

The answer may come even while I am opening up to know the guidance needed. Or it may come a day or two later. No matter how long it takes, I remain open all the way through, until I receive the full message.

For guidance that seems to take longer than the immediate moment, it is important to remain open in a waiting mode, listening, and keeping the space open in inquiry.

Perhaps it hasn't yet registered that you are receiving divine information, but it is happening. When we ask a question, sometimes the answer does not seem to come right away. It may come when you are in the shower, relaxing in bed, driving, or even the next day or two. It may come through hearing someone say something which has nothing to do with what you asked your intuition, but through that experience, you receive an intuition that answers your question for Love. It may come as you silence doubt about your ability to receive divine intuition.

Whether you initiate divine contact or it comes to you on its own, once you begin tuning in to Love and asking a question, expecting an answer, and waiting and listening, you will find yourself doing it more and more often because of its immense value. With practice, you will become more intuitive, convinced of its accuracy, and be able to lean on it all the time. The results are powerful and healing, not only for yourself, but for blessing others as well.

How do you know if it is your own thought or a divinely intuited thought?

As you practice tuning in to Love – asking a question, opening up to know, remaining open as the guidance gently unfolds – you will increasingly become aware of how the guidance arrives. Love's intuited messages may inform you before you even ask, or they may come more as a very vague, remote feeling of possibility which you slowly become aware of. As you focus on going within and evaluate the times and ways it comes, you will become more familiar with how you receive Love's healing intuited messages.

Sometimes I ask for guidance on a specific subject and the answer may be so unexpected that I question if I listened correctly. In such times, I remain open for confirmation. Occasionally I ask for a sign, even a little sign or thought, or a new sense of things that helps me to know. Of course, we want to avoid asking and then forgetting to remain open. It doesn't work if you forget to listen.

Even when you are not asking or intuiting, you are always receiving divine messages every moment and every hour.

Intuitions are non-stop communications from Love and they heal. These messages are forever available, broadcasting to you, whether or not you are listening.

The benefit comes only if and when you tune in. It will take effort on your part to learn how to intuit and then how to trust what is coming to you from Love's healing place. Your quiet patience and efforts to practice intuition will help you more than anything to learn this. Your deep desire to know God is your teacher on intuition.

Sometimes we want something so much that we assume that this is intuition. This takes careful discernment. Is what you want also Love's will or your own will – which may even be in conflict with Love?

Staying wide open without attachment to outcome helps Love's plan to become visible sooner. Your own will may be a wonderful way you think you can be blessed. But if it did not come from intuition, it could be wishful on your part. Then you will need to ask yourself which is more important – your wish or Love's? Which do you most trust?

The only way of knowing if your desire is in alignment with Love is to know that you intuited it from Love. If you aren't sure, then ask Love again until it is clear or you sense it is confirmed in your mind or gut feeling. As you listen with full humility and openness, you will know.

What if I disagree with Love's will for me?

It's not about getting the answer that you want or fulfilling your personal desires. Let's pause here to discuss this extremely important point.

Sometimes I hear my clients resist when I say, "Let's trust Love's perfect will to solve this." They may think that Love's will is going to be harmful, hurtful, or create loss for them.

If you find yourself resisting when you think of Love's will, let's challenge why you resist.

First of all, you do not understand what you are trusting if you resist the divine.

It is important for us, when we pray, not to pray for outcomes such as a house to sell or more money in the bank. It may be that Love has designed a far better outcome than you have outlined as your solution. It may be that, in order for you to go to the next step in your spiritual progress, you need to express patience or joy or understanding.

So if the house did sell, you might miss Love's bigger lesson. Love is always full of wonderful solutions, and many times they come in surprises far better than we could dream up.

Let's go past superficial, ignorant views on this all important subject and look a little deeper at the very nature of Love. Think about it. Do you really think that Love would ever harm you or want to?

Think of someone you deeply love – your child, spouse, parent, friend, or pet. When you deeply love someone, you always want the best possible thing for this person. Now are you beginning to understand the nature of Love?

If it were in your power to empower them or give them every advantage or solve their problems, you would do it if you could. A parent is tirelessly wanting everything for his or her child – the best possible education, friends, opportunities, longevity, health, adoration, purpose, protection, peace, love, and joy. The list is endless!

You are now in touch with Love's will. Pause and reflect on this. Isn't your love for your loved one a wonderful and accurate measurement of divine Love's love for you?

Frankly, if divine Love was any less than the love we give to our loved ones, Love would not be worthy of our worship and prayer. Please think way outside the box and shift higher in your concept of Love's will.

Healing is about growing and expanding and lifting into higher concepts of yourself as divine. Divine Love is infinite in its desire to bless you! Often what you may think is your greatest blessing is not what Love thinks. Love may have a better plan. Not one of suffering or misery, but one of enriched learning, fulfillment, and goodness.

When you ask Love to fulfill its infinite will to bless you, you are relaxing in the arms of Love's care. This is practicing trust in divine guidance. This is what intuition is for. This is what healing looks like. This alone creates a life of healing, oneness, and deep, inner peace.

Angels appeared as a voice during an accident

One rainy morning after dropping off my daughter at school, I headed home and rounded a curve only to see a red pick-up truck coming down the hill toward me and totally out of control. It was obvious we were going to hit. I knew it was only seconds away.

At the time this occurred, I was in prayer. Before I could even form a question or summon Love for help, we collided. About one second before the impact, I heard a sound that said, "The Lord is all present." The sound filled my car with a presence.

I knew that it wasn't me. I don't speak like that. With the sound came a profound assurance of wellness and protection. The red truck and I hit head on. Though my brand new car was a total wreck, unsalvageable, and his truck was also totally wrecked, both of us walked away from our wreckages! Isn't that astonishing? But natural to Love.

I discovered later, when I got home, that my little finger was broken. So grateful to be alive and having been protected by the Voice, I was without any fear and merely made a simple splint and prayed, remembering who I was – my Highest Self identity.

Over the course of the next two weeks, which was about how long the healing took, I assured myself that I had never lapsed from divine Love or its state of wholeness. The prayers were confident and always guided by Love, and my finger was completely healed.

What talks us out of our intuition

We live in a culture that is rational. We tend to believe what we see and can prove. Anything outside this box is doubtful. Yet for centuries, indigenous people have successfully survived by using their intuition along with their intellect. Intuition often saved them from harm or annihilation.

We are conditioned to believe that the answer always lies outside of us. Intuition is exactly the opposite. It is the answer that always lies within you.

Practice intuition on "claims" of loss

One way to practice and develop your intuition is on lost items. Since Love is all present and always available to us, Love offers an information bank that we can readily access anytime.

Whenever I think I have lost my car keys, lipstick, papers, or anything else, I do the usual search. If it doesn't show up, instead of going into a panic, declaring that I have lost something, I have an entirely different routine. The first goal is not to act out that something is lost. The second goal is to remain calm while reminding myself that I am Highest Self which is incapable of ignorance. All knowingness is mine. There is nothing I do not know. There is nothing I cannot recall in my all knowingness. In divine reality, my consciousness is never confused, but always orderly and accessible with all intelligence.

Usually, before I even sit down to begin tuning in, an image will appear, showing me the location of the lost object or causing me to recall the lost thought. But the issue is not how long it takes. I keep door number one – Love's healing – open at all times. Staying open to Love's messages is all we really want or need for healing.

In divine intuition, we check in with the spiritual senses and rely on these intuitive senses rather than the problem that appears to be true.

This same process works successfully whether you are intuiting for car keys, a love mate, a job, a place to live, food, finances, health matters, or any other outcome. You are merely acknowledging your need for divine guidance and re-connecting with an identity that you believe you have lost.

Your true self, your divine Highest Self, is whole, complete, and incapable of loss. You are merely reminding yourself of what is true, according to Love.

For lost objects, I also come to my defense by reminding myself that I am not disorderly, confused, guilty, wrong, careless, forgetful, aging, neglectful, or worthy of condemnation.

This is usually the mental crew that works against our finding what appears to be lost. Instead, I affirm that I am orderly, innocent, clear, all knowing, diligent, unlapsing, remembering, ageless, caring, and alert. And I rest in expectation, knowing that, as the mental crew of opposition leaves, this will bring forth what appeared to be lost.

If the situation is a financial loss, it is no different. Your stand is that your Highest Self is exempt from all losses. You may find, surprisingly, that some appearances of loss may actually wind up as gain.

We need to re-present our Highest Selves to ourselves every day many times. The practice of staying in your Highest Self creates a pattern or habit. My entire days are filled with staying tuned in as long and as often as possible.

Whether I am in a movie, at a dinner party, around many people, quietly taking a practice call, or in a personally stressful situation, I am mostly tuned in to see what Love is telling me. I often thank myself for having the good sense to do this too. It really makes me happy and it will you too.

Ask Love

This is the key to all healing. I repeat, this is the key to all healing. Simply ask Love.

Ask Love all day long and all night long, whenever you think of it. Ask Love – in order to understand, know, see, and open you to Love's healing way. Get yourself on the same page as Love. Be with Love. Ask. Ask. Ask.

Whenever I begin to pray or intuit in a healing case, I do not assume that I know what is going on, ever, not for a second. I know that I need Love to tell me and I wait for Love. I ask.

You can begin this wonderful way of living that will bring power beyond your wildest imagination to every healing. Ask Love what you need to know and understand. You will find yourself with Love's infinite intelligence and wisdom unfolding to you, slowly and gently. Stay open. Keep asking.

We are never begging or pleading. Healing work is never tense. As you relax in trust, confidence, and even curiosity, you will come to know everything you need to know in order to bring forth healing.

Listen keenly to the angels

Love's angel thoughts, by the zillions, are with you every moment, always present and available.

The angels bring a plan for you to be healed and they create the perfect condition for every healing. Opening us to new visions, they prepare the way for healing. Love's angels show us the way of healing as they both comfort and encourage, lifting us from the depths.

As divine messengers, they bring light and understanding through our intuition. Their intention is to direct healing for your well being and life direction. Their work is wonderful! Never fear angels. They are your best friends. I passionately love them!

Entire armies of angels are brought to you in behalf of healing. These angels are always loving you with a desire to bless you and with full power to heal you. Never believe for even a moment that it is Love's will for you not to be healed.

Never doubt your divine right to be healed of anything and everything. Angels offer a world of healing. They are completely capable of healing you at this and every moment. They bring truth. They awaken you to a higher realm of reality. All that is needed from you is your full receptivity.

Ask yourself, "To what extent am I fully receptive to divine guidance?" This is the all-important question. Angels are available to you. Are you also available to them?

We answer, "Of course!" But are you available on *their* terms?

Often when I awaken in the middle of the night, I may be awake briefly or for several hours.

During this quiet time, I turn to Love to feel its healing Presence while holding the space open, ready for Love's healing information and influence. I allow my desire for Love to swell into enormity. For example, the spirit of my prayer may be: "I want you, Love, to be made manifest in my conscious experience as I lie here. I am filled with desire for Your Presence."

While lying there, I imagine what thoughts Love must be thinking. I claim those wonderful intelligent, productive thoughts for myself as Love's emanation. I may not know the specific thought at that moment, but that is okay. I imagine being in Love's infinitely perfect arrangement with my purpose performing itself at the highest level.

By remaining open to Love, I eventually feel a sense of calm, peace, and wellness. I may also have healing insights, inspiration, and intuition. Many ideas in this book were written by awakening in the night and writing in the dark what Love wanted me (and us) to know.

Ask Love all day long and during the night as well. Ask Love for a visit. Even though Love is already with you, as you quiet the material senses that keep your mind stirred, you will more and more experience Love's healing presence and know its messages. It will feel like a visit from divine Love.

In order to establish a new habit, it is helpful to attach it to your daily routine.

For example, we all know in advance that we will be choosing what to wear and eat, turning on the ignition or handing the bus ticket to the bus driver, walking down a hallway, going to the bathroom, waiting for someone, and on and on. Decide now, that during all these empty moments – and others of your choosing – you will turn to Love and ask for a visit, keeping open the space for the healing presence of divine Love.

Even if this is all that occurs during these moments, you will be greatly comforted. You will be like a toddler who looks for mom or dad and only needs to touch her skirt or his pants leg. Then you will know all is well. You are not alone. Leaning on Love for help has an enormous healing impact on our days and overall lives because it takes away fear and brings in healing. Later, at longer intervals, you can listen even more and receive specific information needed.

The healing power of intuition and receptivity combined

I am deeply impressed with some people whose receptivity sets forth a grand expectation of immediate healing. In my practice, I see this in varying degrees. Some who call are more receptive than others.

I flood with healing treatment to the degree someone is receptive. If they are really tuned in with humility and expectation for healing from our work together, healing can present itself almost instantly. If they are not, they will most likely interrupt me during a verbal healing treatment. Or sometimes, in someone's silence, there is a feeling of resistance. I can always feel it.

Here are two examples of wide-open receptivity:

A woman called and described herself as very ill. She was suffering from a high fever and was in bed. I felt her receptivity for spiritual healing and her expectation to have things shifted as a result of our conversation. I could feel the divine Presence as I gave her treatment. She was with me every word, hanging on. I could feel it. I am deeply impressed with this level of receptivity. It inspires much healing! These are some of my most joyful times in the healing practice.

She recalled later what I said that most helped her on our healing call. I told her that, with most receptive people who called, they would be healed in less than twenty four hours. But because of her receptivity, I expected her healing within the next twenty minutes!

I had forgotten that I said that to her. I don't usually make such projections about outcome. However, in her case, because of her beautiful, pure receptivity and expectation for healing, I was led to say those words to her. The words pushed themselves out of my mouth. Angels.

She called later to tell me it was within twenty minutes after our talk that she was completely healed. There's the power of receptivity and expectation combined.

Here's another example. A man called with an abscessed tooth and was in great pain. I recall his tremendous receptivity. Again, it felt like he was hanging on to every word that I spoke. Each word poured out of me straight from divine Love. We were one. I told him, if he was not vastly improved within an hour, to please call me again.

I did not hear from him again that day. At a later date, he told me that within two or three minutes after we hung up, the pain left him entirely and he was free of the problem. Isn't that wonderful? Doesn't this show the power of healing we are dealing with? This same power is available to you as well.

Open yourself wide to divine intuition and receive freely from Love's angels pouring out healing for you.

Never try to time a healing. They come according to our receptivity and the divine awakening within. Whether or not a healing is immediate, there is always healing progress occurring whenever we listen for heavenly intuition.

Sometimes it feels like we need oceans of healing and yet we only receive tiny sips. Each sip creates an eventual tidal wave. Your beautiful receptivity will bring this forward. Remain open to Love at all times and practice your openness continually.

Intuition exercise

Here are a few simple steps you can take in order to practice your intuition. You may want to come back to this page each day until you make the experience a wonderful, new healing habit.

First, sit comfortably and relax. Once you feel restful, begin to tune in. Go to your deepest place. Trust that you can ask for this. Assume that your inner knowing and wisdom are there. Then ask a simple question of Love concerning a problem that concerns you.

You might ask:

- What do I need to be aware of that I may not presently know?
- What is Love thinking?

- What is Love leading me to know?
- What is Love leading me to do?

Pause in stillness. Check to see that you are entirely open, listening for Love's answer. Keep listening quietly. Hold the listening space open to receive the answer until you actually receive it. Don't judge the information or your ability to intuit. Acknowledge with thanks whatever you receive.

Acknowledgement is a wonderful way for you to consciously register that your effort at intuition worked. It is important to give gratitude for all blessings – big and small – to keep your heart open and remember your wonderful, true Source.

There are no wrong questions to ask Love. You may develop your own ways of asking. It isn't words as much as the attitude of receptivity, openness, and wanting. It is good to have an imploring attitude of inquiry. I really want to know and I let it be known in my consciousness that I am now asking and waiting for the answer, imploring the answer to be known immediately by me. At times, I place great pressure on my consciousness to be the divine knower that it is created to be. I do this with enthusiasm and without any tension or stress.

Superstition does not come into it. It is not a question of getting on Love's good side or doing Love a favor in exchange for healing. Spiritual healing is totally outside the realm of superstition.

As you practice intuition more and more each day and evening, asking Love for guidance on all things, you learn that you have within you a perfect and blessed ability to know all things that Love wants you to know – available to you always.

Love's spiritual senses

We are accustomed to relying on the material senses for our reality. We tend to most believe what our eyes see and what we hear, touch, smell, and taste. We rely on these superficial material senses for our entire reality.

Yet when we turn to the intuitive spiritual senses to check in with reality, we find that the intuitive spiritual senses often contradict what we see, hear, feel, and believe.

The material senses cause us to believe that Love is the exception, instead of the rule. The material senses – the opposite of spiritual senses – cause us to ignore Love as the one reality.

Outweighing the problem using the spiritual senses

Another word for spiritual intuition is spiritual sense. You could say that, in the areas you need healing, what you really need is a clearer sense of Love's vision and plan for you – Love's sense of the healing, Love's sense of reality.

We tend to sweep over reality, like "Oh, I know all about reality." Really? Can you describe Truth in as full detail as you can your problems? In most cases, until you can outweigh your problem with Love's understanding, you will continue to have the problem. You need the spiritual senses – Love's intuited guidance – for this.

The moment you turn to Love for healing, you have all this on your side. You've turned to the One who most loves you, most wants to offer you comfort and healing, most wants to show you what is the best thing to think, say, or do under the circumstances, and the One that is providing you with all blessings if you will only tune in and listen.

It may sound like I am saying that you and Love are two separate beings. I am not. But there is a path that brings us into the realization of our true oneness and that path is through intuition. All healing depends on it. Otherwise, you are blindly asking a god – way out there somewhere – to come and save you and heal you. In reality, God, or Love is already within you, operating as a law of healing and perfect action to advantage you every moment throughout eternity.

Healing is inspired

All spiritual healing comes from Love's inspiration. Healers are among the most inspired people on earth because they are continually listening to angel messages. This creates a great deal of strength, power, insight, and happiness for their personal lives. This same inspiration is available to you.

Ask yourself:

- Are my thoughts inspired by Love?
- Is this prayer inspired by Love?
- Is this affirmation inspired by Love?
- Is this meditation inspired by Love?
- Is my life inspired by Love?

In your healing work, you can always expect that, when you tune in to Love and are open, willing, and receptive, Love will respond with inspiration.

Love's Niagara Falls is flowing with healing thoughts for you. Allow Love's healing inspiration to flow through you – through your thoughts, feelings, body, and your entire life experience. Let Love's healing inspiration fill your entire being. This is how spiritual healing takes place. It is the fresh, healing inspiration of Love operating through you. Love is your very presence, inspired!

Go forth as the presence of inspired Love. Realize that this living Love presence is your true identity. Embody the fact that your Love presence is a healing presence to yourself and to all who come into your Love atmosphere. Be at one with its healing power, which acts as a quickening to all healing. Think of yourself as the Voice and Message of Love.

Intuiting Love is a wonderful beginning to the practice of spiritual healing. Now we will take this further and unpack how you can experience this at deep levels every day, through meditation, so that you can fully access the healing understanding and power that you need.

Chapter 5

The Sacred Space
of Meditation

A mind that is quiet. This is the purpose of meditation. A still mind offers a fertile soil for rich healing and growth. Can you still your mind?

Most of us enter our days and moments at a great disadvantage. Our minds are preoccupied, unsettled, and wandering. We have frustrations, bottled up anger, fears, worries, and unaddressed needs, with our focus fogged.

What do you think your life would be like if you spent a period of time each morning or evening with your mind quiet – experiencing open mental space without any jumpy nervousness whatsoever? Your daily meditation is the one thing each day that can set the tone for your entire day and positively effect everything.

Meditation is healing.

The healing power of a quiet moment

The mind needs stillness in order to experience maximum intelligence, clarity, and focus. When the mind is racing, it is full of conflicting, unresolved messages. It becomes distracted and it is then difficult to focus on meaningful goals, outlooks, and intuitions for healing solutions. It is hard to wade through daily activities and events with a mind that is stressed, trying to think its clearest and most intelligent thoughts while lacking peace within. Meditation offers a way you can truly advantage yourself in maximum ways. If you are on a spiritual path, meditation is indispensable.

We spend only a fraction of our lives in the Highest Self while the vast majority of our time is spent processing life's daily activities.

A tiny fraction of your time, spent in meditation, can direct your entire life purpose and destiny, bringing success, opportunities, healings, power, and bliss – connecting you with Love every moment.

Imagine your day filled with inner peace. Your natural calm, joy, intelligence, inner wisdom, and happiness could surface and become available and present. Your awareness would spread to others around you and you would become a healing support to them as well as to yourself.

What's so great about quietness of the mind? In quietness you can:

- Receive divine guidance and vision to carry out your highest life path possibility. How important and healing is that?
- Realize you are never alone. Receive the infinite comfort of this.
- Come into oneness with all being.
- Discover what is perfect about this moment. Experience that the only presence is now and the only reality is Love's present one.
- Receive a key word, image, or inspiration for the day, keeping you uplifted and guided by Love.
- Flow in Love.
- Let go of "monkey mind" – jumpiness, nervousness, futurizing, or dwelling on the past.
- Clear out mental cobwebs and negativity.
- Gain clarity and inner peace.

- Discover what Soul is wanting to birth through you.

Meditation unites us with Love

In order to experience healing with Love, we need to become more like Love. When we become quiet and still the mind, we can then unite with the thoughts of Love that we so long to feel. They were within you all along. We can then experience our true divine Self and divine reality.

During meditative quiet time, we allow the mind to become still so love and inspiration can flow. In my personal experience, when my mind is jumping around, Love's healing messages are stressed, even giving the feeling I need to hurry. In such times, every thought has to push its way through to the surface in order to be known. This is a stressful way to heal.

When meditating, however, as we become still and open ourselves to Love, then healing thoughts can dawn. This is a happy time of inner peace and reflection. Thoughts are sorted out naturally as you sit in quiet peace and allow Love's presence to prevail. You can learn about yourself and better manage your life with higher choices after reflecting on what is going on in your life.

Meditation provides an avenue for positive change and growth. Reflection and growth are positive barriers to many illnesses. They act as preventive medicine. Reflection offers "God moments" where important solutions to problems can unfold.

Meditation is also an excellent practice of the Highest Self. During a meditative period, we stay tuned, listening for information, guidance, comfort, peace, understanding, and healing. Our main job is to stay still, quiet, and peaceful so Love's thoughts can become known and felt within us. Thus we awaken to our Highest Self.

The power of a simple meditation

One morning while attending a conference, I meditated on my identity as "the radiant light of infinite Love." Since the conference was intense and there was little time to meditate, this simple meditation unfolded while in the shower. Here is the power of a simple meditation brought by Love.

I walked to breakfast contemplating this simple meditation and ate breakfast with others while I thought of myself and others as "the radiant light of infinite Love" and attended the conference with this meditation in mind. My simple intention was to stay centered in Love and see all others as the presence of Love.

It wasn't hard. I spent small moments adoring and cherishing our identities as sourced from living Love.

This meditation meant a great deal to me. Not only did it bring deep, rich love to my own day, but the Love packed into this meditation also brought enormous healing to others at the conference.

By the morning break, a woman came up to me and asked what I did as a spiritual healer. While I answered, I sensed her inner plea for help. She explained that she had been suffering from intense headache pains for three months from a severe infection. She was taking medication, but it was failing to relieve her of pain for more than short spans of time.

As she spoke, I thought of us surrounded in the enormous power of healing Love. She interrupted herself in the midst of describing her problem to ask, "What are you doing? My headache is going away!"

I shared Love's message with her. "You are the radiant light of infinite Love." Her eyes welled with tears. As I held her in Love's embrace, I again thought of our true, divine identity as Love's own expression. We hugged as she said, "My headache is completely gone."

What a moment we had shared! We were in the presence of living Love! We were identifying ourselves as this very Presence. The result was healing. I saw her again, days later, at the end of the conference. She said the pain never returned and she had been healed from the day we spoke. There were others that day who were also healed by this same powerful meditation. This healing effect is typical of divine Love's presence.

The Love we represent begs to be more fully shared and realized. When we love well – deeply and thoroughly – our natural desire is to not only stay in Love's presence, but also to go to the place that most hurts and bring comfort and healing.

It is time for us to remember our roots in Love. We come from divine Love. We are the ambassadors of Love's radiant light. As we recall who we are in Love, our spiritual identity becomes the medicine of Soul and food for the hungering heart.

The forces of anti-meditation

There are many forces in our lives that pull us away from meditation. For example, most news is anti-meditative. It is not healing.

Newspapers, magazines, and television report sensational stories with constant repetition of the same disturbing headline stories over and over all day.

What percent of the news do you really need? Feeding off excess bad news is unhealthy. We can learn to watch with an alert detachment, or review news online to receive selective news stories.

I usually tune in to headline news for the first ten minutes. If it is disaster, I will catch the simple version of the report and remain in quietness about it. My compassion often turns to prayer or blessing for the danger or suffering in the news. I do not dwell on the news stations. We cannot be meditative if we dwell on daily dangers, murders, robberies, and violence.

Our culture is training us to become addicted to being excited and unsettled. We've become addicted to sensationalism.

Watching the news means you will hear a deliberate vocabulary of words like disaster, accident, tragedy, violence, and murder. We're fed this in large daily doses!

This creates insecurity and anxiety and is not conducive to inner peace.

Most commercials are anti-meditative

Advertising codes us with suggestions of "You need! You want! Go buy!"

They leave us with the message of our inadequacy and unacceptableness to society unless we purchase the product they are selling. Companies spend millions of dollars to convince you without a doubt that you need their product.

They make it their top priority to persuade you through repetition, entertainment, celebrity or role model influence, intimidation, humor, or any other way their marketing has proven best gets you to buy their product.

You are a focused study for these companies to learn how to prove to you that you need and want their products. Their entire advertising dollars depend on success through controlling your thinking and behavior. Commercials also show problems to convince you that these problems are your own and they can only be solved through your purchase of the product or service.

Multi-tasking is anti-meditative

Doing several things at once creates a fully occupied, busy mind which is under stress to perform simultaneously. This sends a message to us that we are in a hurry or under pressure.

By contrast, one task at a time, thoughtfully done with Love's honoring, creates a powerful energy to flow through your day with harmony, peace, and calm tranquility. Slowing down has great rewards for inner peace.

My 3 a.m. meditation

As mentioned before, I often awaken in the night and view this time as a quiet Love visit. It is often the most powerful meditative healing work I do. Here is how I use meditation to make these moments holy and healing.

I simply lie there in stillness and quiet. The only mental activity I do is "hold the space open" for Love's healing presence. I do this consciously every moment, as much as I can.

When my mind starts wandering or worrying, I still hold the space open for Love and allow fear and disturbing thoughts to be in the background, eventually drowned out by the presence of Love. It doesn't happen right away. Meditation cultivates patience. It is well worth the wait, too. Meanwhile, I focus on Love.

Meditation is transitioning from a state of unsettled thinking to a state of calm and inner stillness.

In my meditation, I become quiet. Then I become aware of thoughts. I don't tell myself these are *my* thoughts. They are just thoughts, that's all. I try not to become attached to them as they unfold.

Then I begin consciously holding the space open for Love's healing presence to be experienced by me. I acknowledge that Love is already there with me and messaging to me. I merely have to quiet my mind's busy fluttering thoughts in order to hear what Love is messaging.

As you sit or lie in stillness and become receptive to Love, and hold the space open, busy thoughts recede into the background. You are transitioning to a place of deep peace, reality, and healing.

It is amazing how successful this is. Once my mind is quiet, I may choose a couple of different ways of expressing meditation.

One is just to sustain the quiet pause and remain still. Enjoying the stillness, I try to stay in the present moment. This in itself is a successful meditation.

Or, once I become quiet and still, I may use meditation to reflect on my life and see what Love is saying about it.

Or I may ask Love for an answer to a problem. I may ask for guidance. Then I stay in the open space, waiting. Time is no longer a factor. I have already decided that no matter how long it takes to receive an answer – hours, days, weeks – I will wait. And I will continue to hold the space open as I transition to the awareness of Love's healing.

Fortunately, it rarely takes a long period of time to receive an answer. If my question is complex, I may find that Love is teaching me through stages of understanding. If the question is simple, I may know the answer quickly, even instantly.

For complex cases in my healing practice, I listen for long periods in order to understand the nature of the problem beyond the face of it – the healing behind the healing. And I listen deeply for the infrastructure to the healing. The value of meditation is inestimable.

In the middle of the night, however, my primary goal is to still and quiet my mind so I can feel the inner peace and know that Love is present with me.

The effect of this is deeply grounding and assuring. This is healing.

I meditate every day. It is hard to know when I am not meditating since I am nearly always listening to Love's interpretation to everything in my life.

A meditative life is filled with pauses

Each day between events, goings and comings, projects, and activities, I pause to check in with Love. A simple practice of pause is powerful to bring you back into the moment and the presence of quiet stillness. It is important to practice peaceful energy and to remind yourself that you are never alone. Love is always here with you.

For example, after working an hour or so at the desk, I may walk through the house in a pause. I may refresh my glass of water and slowly drink. If the calls have come in with short intervals in between, I will pause after a few of the calls and perhaps take a deep breath at my desk, in restfulness and mindfulness. I may ring my singing bell to remind me of the clarity of peace present. I may glance at the small candle flickering, lighting up my desk space in effortless peace. I may go outside and smell one of the heavenly flowers which grow profusely outside my office. Or smell a flower on my desk. All of these are lovely pauses. I do them all day long because they are enjoyable.

Pauses create peace and often bring wisdom and healing.

Pauses keep me peaceful, balanced, and attuned to Love's healing messages. After I am engaged in activities such as driving in the car or doing errands, I pause when I come home. I may pause between each activity as well. This avoids stress as much as possible and allows inner peace to continue without interruption.

Contrary to what you may think, pauses do not slow down productivity. They actually make you more efficient and far happier.

In addition to bringing you back to the present moment, pauses also create moments for reflection where you can consider things that occurred earlier or things to come. You can make new and better decisions based on what you learn during pauses, and grow from these moments of enormous potential learning.

Toddlers can learn to pause

I taught my daughter pauses when she was a toddler. We balanced big activity with little activity.

For example, following her big outdoor play, she would come inside for a quieter activity, such as having refreshments, or doing an art project, reading, or quiet play. It is common for children to overplay and then come inside with stress, excess hunger, and an inability to quiet themselves. It often leads to discord and tears.

I don't recall the children who played at our house ever suffering from these imbalances. Children need to be taught pauses and balanced activity. They need peace. It is just as important for children to learn to peacefully quiet themselves as it is for adults.

From the time my daughter started talking, she was aware of my need to be quiet at times. And almost always when we got on the freeway for long distances, such as twenty minute drives, I would request some quiet time, even if for a few moments.

For example, after we chatted for awhile, I would tell her I needed to be quiet and asked if she would be quiet with me. She never seemed to mind. In fact, I think she enjoyed it, too. This was always done with love. I often spoke to her afterwards to share what

Love told me during my quiet moments and sometimes it would be about her. She liked it.

As she observed my model of meditation, she found comfort with her own company and our shared silence. Far from making her a dull person, these pauses helped develop her creativity and her ability to be quiet herself. Today, as an adult, she incorporates daily meditation and spiritual healing in her life, finding it indispensable to her peace and happiness.

Living from an enlightened state

The goal is for your life to come from the very best of yourself, from your enlightened state, to reach your full divine potential. Otherwise, the day's random mixed bag of ups and downs are liable to overwhelm your Highest Self and prevent you from fulfilling and actualizing your highest life purpose and Self. Meditation can help us do this.

To be healers, we need to be experts at connecting to Love through quietness or meditation. And the good news for all of us is that learning to meditate is easy to do once we break through the resistance. Once you discover that meditation is not only pleasant, but indispensable to your day's happiness and well being, you will find healing easy and enjoyable.

Find your Love note and start singing

Every day, I draw on Love's healing inspiration. It may be inspiration from a book written by an authentic spiritual teacher and thinker, a Scripture, the Vedas, a hymn, a poem, or something that Love told me.

Once I gain a simple, powerful healing thought, I use it throughout the day. In fact, I find that my entire day will come into alignment to that simple powerful thought. The day's mix of drama, people, actions, conversations, feelings, and perceptions all rise to be attuned to the highest note of Truth. I am singing my highest and most beautiful note all day while allowing everything in my day to rise and harmonize at the highest level I am singing.

For example, one day I found myself singing the note of Light, which is a powerful, recurring theme in my healing practice.

The inspiration came through divine intuition that Love is radiating a light – powerful and beautiful. I thought of this Light as being everywhere at once, all-encompassing and all present. I could see that each of us are a light of Love. As I pondered this, I began to see myself and those close to me as Love's lights, brightly lit and radiating a light of purity, intelligence, power, and joy.

As the day progressed, I identified everyone who came to my thought as being filled with Love's Light, and not with darkness. I saw that each of us are free of illusions of dark thoughts, gloom, doom, dark places, dark spells, feeling alone, forsaken, or abused. I applied this to the people in poverty, enslavement, terror, war, prisons, and refugee camps. I only saw Light surrounding them and filling them.

I also applied the Light to clients who called, assuring them and awakening them to the truth of their being, their precious and needed light. I reminded them of their identity as a Light bearer, a child of the Light. What remarkable, joyful missions we, as Lights, have been assigned! And we are prepared and ordained to be successful every moment as rays of Love's light. We are Light healers, empowered.

Think of how, when we come into a dark room and turn on the light switch, the darkness is gone. The light is then present in the room which before seemed to be filled with darkness. The light is sufficient to dispel the illusion of darkness, in every case. We are that room, lit. We are the Light, lighting up the world, ourselves, and the entire planet. I sang the note of the Light.

You, too, can find your Love note and start singing it. Sing it with all your heart. Let your song heal the world. Maintaining a spiritual theme during your day is a powerful action for healing.

When someone calls me for several days, or for longer periods of time, you would be surprised at how little of our time is used to discuss the problem.

Generally, I ask for a brief progress update report and then I inquire about their state of mind. "What are you primarily thinking about during the day? What spiritual thought or theme plays in your mind? Are you holding pictures of the problem? Fearing and dreading it? Or are you holding pictures and thoughts of the spiritual solution, outside the problem and healing you?" This is the report I am looking for. This will tell me everything about the healing progress we are making.

I help people to organize their thoughts and stick with the spiritual theme. Like a powerful lawyer arguing her case, I pour in healing truth to outweigh the problem and assert its authority and supremacy.

I also encourage people to do more of this on their own after our phone conversation. Maintain a spiritual theme of daily, fresh inspiration. This is a key to every healing. And this is a key to living a spiritual life. The sooner this occurs, the sooner the healing comes. Willingness to do this is powerful to bring forth their healing.

If you want to get on the same page as your healing, begin here. Many times, the mere willingness to do this brings forth immediate and full healing. This is certainly the path of spiritual healing and it gives a great education in how healing works.

Decide on a place

First of all, for a successful meditation practice, decide on a place to meditate. It can be your bed, desk, a comfortable chair, on the floor, in a corner, or outside in nature. Choose anywhere it is guaranteed that you can be quiet, comfortable, and uninterrupted for the period of time you wish to meditate.

It is helpful to have your meditation place in a room where you can close the door and be alone. Designating a place to meditate is vital to the success of your daily practice.

You also need a place to stack your inspirational literature and items you may want with you for meditation. This can be by your bedside, at your desk, in another room, or in the corner or closet. It needs to be accessible.

Your stack can consist of items such as books, affirmation cards, spiritual publications, tapes, a personal journal, and a pad of writing paper. Then, during quiet times, you can select inspirational readings. Your main objective is to keep inspiring spiritual thoughts flowing and prominent in your mind on a daily basis.

Once you still your mind, you can then reflect, study, renew, refresh, and listen to Love's messages – even for 10-15 minutes. New habits start slowly. These are healing minutes. Even sitting still and bringing your mind to quietness is healing. This can lead to wonderful healings, especially when done on a regular basis. Remember why you are being quiet. It is to still your mind so you can experience peace and listen to Love!

There is no perfect time to meditate

The fact is, the place and time to meditate will only happen if you initiate it. It won't come to you. The main reason people do not meditate is either that they do not know its value or that they procrastinate doing it. Don't procrastinate another moment. Do it today. Then do it again tomorrow. Then again the next day.

Do it until you can journal the benefits and consciously build it into your life. It will lead your life in powerful healing ways. Even if you start out meditating a minute a day, meditation will shape your happiness and well being more than I could possibly describe. Even little sips of Love are awesome in nourishing healing. Spiritual healing is dependent on meditation. It is pure joy to discover the power of these healing moments. Meditation is a discipline that leads to enormous healing.

On my desk, on the right side, is always a stack of books, articles, or tapes. I don't feel obligated to read them. I only read when Love leads me. Sometimes I may remove the book or tape that I no longer feel inspired to read or listen to. Think of the stack as a well of fresh water and, when you are thirsty, you can dip into the well. There is never guilt if you don't drink the water.

Or you can get rid of your stack without ever having read a word of it. Do only what Love is telling you to do. This is the meditative practice, completely guided by Love, and only Love.

I have many books, but unless Love directs me, and unless I feel led, I do not read them. My only obligation is to divine Love.

Once you sit in stillness, you can choose to either remain quiet, holding open the space for listening to Love, or you can focus attention on inspiring healing thoughts. See what you most need. Each day may be a little different.

For your meditation, you can choose to stay in the present moment, quiet your mind, listen for holy thoughts, or study something spiritual. Your purpose is to listen intuitively to The Holy One Who Heals All Through Love.

Scott's meditative place

Scott has a home office which is the hub of his very active business life and he has oriented himself for meditation in a few simple ways. Each morning or evening, he does a yoga practice in his office, followed by meditation sitting on a floor cushion on his yoga mat. Once he sits on his cushion, his entire office is transformed into a meditative center.

Even after meditation, during the day when he comes in and out of the room doing business, he sees the meditative cushion set aside on the floor and his mat rolled up in the corner, and he is constantly reminded of his Highest Self's thoughts and feels more at peace. Sometimes he even leaves his mat unrolled to remind him of his Higher Self as he steps over it into "work."

From Scott's and my spiritual practice, we share daily insights, outcomes, and inspirations from our meditations as a way of staying in touch with each other's hearts. It also keeps us in constant touch with our life purposes and Highest Selves. We love sharing what Love messages to us!

An environment of order

When you sit still to meditate in your designated place at the same time each day, it also helps to have things tidy around you. The mind tends to focus on messes or clutter. In meditation, we accomplish serenity through clarity and stillness of the mind.

If you feel you can't stop to clean up the area where you meditate, go ahead and meditate anyway. Let nothing stand in the way of your meditating.

Once you establish a place to meditate, decide on a time as well as the length of time to meditate. The same time each day is the most helpful in order to establish the habit of meditation. Consistency in meditation is helpful, even if it is for just a short while.

I flow in meditation from the moment I get up. While in the shower, I am holding the space open for Love's healing thoughts, messages, guidance, or focus. At the same time, I am allowing the busy thoughts to go to the background. This seems to be my best way of meditating since it is continual.

Set your intention

As you still your mind, becoming quiet, set your intention on something you wish to heal or what you wish to accomplish in the time allotted. For example, you may want to briefly identify a problem where you can begin listening for a solution. Or you may want to listen for what to have as your intention. Let Love tell you.

You may simply want to use the meditation time to be quiet and still and listen for Love's messages. Let yourself experience inner peace.

You may feel led to meditate with an intention to support a particular person or people of the world, or the state of the world. These are powerful intentions. It is a wonderful step of healing progress to experience the greater love which comes when you open your heart with compassion towards others' sufferings and give love generously during your meditation to help them.

You may need this meditation time for yourself in order to reflect on your life. This is where I begin most meditations.

There are many different approaches to meditation

Yoga practice

Yoga, for example, is excellent for quieting the mind. During or after yoga practice, meditate. It is sometimes helpful to focus on an intention that may come to you from your yoga practice. Sometimes my intention may be to live in the moment. Other times, I love dedicating my practice to the world that all may feel my healing love pour out to them.

Deep breathing meditation

Sometimes I do simple deep breathing exercises while slowly counting the length of inhales and exhales. This is very meditative because it absolutely keeps you in the present moment, which is great for calming the mind.

I begin with a slow inhale through my nose, mentally counting up to three. Then hold the inhale one or two counts. Then exhale to the count of three. Then repeat.

With each completed series, I will increase the count by one breath, all the way up to eight or even ten or more counts. It is important to always breathe with comfort, never straining or needing to gasp for breath. If I am uncomfortable, I may only go up to five or six counts on each inhale and exhale, with a count or two in between the breaths. You can find what is most comfortable for you. Stay relaxed in every breath. Your comfort level will often vary from day to day.

A mind that is still can be in the present moment with Love. A mind that is meditating can do deep spiritual listening and bring forth much healing.

Mindfulness practice

Another approach to meditation is the practice of mindfulness. At varying times during the day, pause to be mindful. Thich Nhat Hahn, a noted Buddhist monk and wonderful author, teaches simple mindfulness sequences such as: "Breathing in, I calm myself. Breathing out, I smile." Slowly repeat this several times. You can practice mindful awareness in the shower, dressing, sitting, eating, and walking.

In every thought and every action in every minute each day, we are influencing and having an effect on each other and the planet, even in far away places. Staying in the moment is so helpful to quiet the mind, feel calm, and get in touch with Love's healing messages.

Transcendental meditation

Many years ago, I practiced transcendental meditation. This is another excellent means of meditation. A couple times a day, I sat in meditation and repeated my mantra (a Sanskrit word) over and over in my mind for about twenty minutes.

During this time, I was told that I would have lots of thoughts coming up. The mind has great resistance to being still. That's okay. I was instructed to let all the thoughts go and simply keep saying the mantra. The results were wonderful. This is very similar to my practice of "holding the space open" for Love when I awake in the middle of the night.

The most obvious effect is that transcendental meditation creates deep relaxation. Dr. Herbert Benson's research for Harvard Medical School shows that TM creates a state of rest even far deeper than sleep, giving the mind and body freedom from stress. One of the many great effects of this is better health and mental clarity, even as you age.

Although I no longer practice TM, I learned that no matter how chatty my mind is, I can always focus on opening to Love. I can sit and quietly wait on Love to move my thought or experience.

Meditative music

Another wonderful meditation pathway is with music. Scott and I often listen to inspired music or chants which quiet our minds and take us to a wonderful place of spiritual joy. Uplifting music can refresh our minds for days and offer enormous healing and joy.

Infinite paths, one peace

I suggest you explore many ways to meditate. My preference as a healer is to simply still myself and, in quietness, go within. This is where I do some of my best listening to Love in order to be guided to heal.

As a healer, I am always seeking to know what Love is telling me. My mind needs to be quiet in order to know this. My desire is great.

I have found that, after almost thirty years of practicing meditation, I can be in the middle of chaos and be perfectly still. Often, for months on end, the majority of calls that come in to my healing practice phone line are calls of crises. Yet I am Love's rock.

My peace, for the most part, is unshakeable, because it is really Love's peace. I use my deep peace to listen to Love in responding to people's problems. The result is enormously healing. Rather than my client and I both going downward to the lowest level of crises, we both rise to the highest level of the place where I keep my consciousness. It only takes one healer and one spiritually receptive person to bring forth healing. I sing Love's healing song.

A meditative life is a harmonious, powerful, healing life. You are tapping into the infinite reservoir of Love for comfort, calmness, understanding, guidance, and healing. You are living an intimate relationship with divine Love. The outcome of your happiness and ability to heal is immeasurable.

I often feel bliss during the day and sometimes for days on end.

I am often in awe of my life experience and the quality of fearlessness that I experience each day. I experience on a regular basis what most people call miracles. Yet miracles are normal to one who meditates with Love. You will see.

You can use meditation to feel the presence of Love within and all around you. You can experience Love's healing presence, guidance, and compassionate care as you know the joy of mental quietness and peace. Over time, the power will astound you. You, too will become a tower of strength and calm.

In summary, to experience sacred meditation:

- Become still.
- Quiet the mind.
- Be in the present moment.
- Hold the space open to Love as you pause.
- Listen and intuit Love.

Meditation prepares the way for deeper healing through prayer, as we will discuss in the next chapter.

Chapter 6

Prayer
that Heals

When my niece was about three years old, she had severe spinal meningitis. The whole family gathered in the hospital corridor that evening, waiting for the professional team of doctors to finish speaking with my brother and sister-in-law. The news was grave.

We were told that she might not make it through the night. And if she did make it through the night, she may have a host of terrible problems such as brain damage and physical disabilities. We felt numb as we listened to the horrible news.

We are from a small town in Arkansas. Everyone knew about Shannon (my namesake). The Presbyterian church, where her family were members, had been praying. Mother sent word to the church about the gravity of the situation.

Moments after we heard the news of Shannon's poor chances for living through the night, the phone in the hospital corridor rang. It was a woman calling from the church to say that a prayer vigil had been organized and the church members would pray all through the night for Shannon. It makes me cry every time I recall this support.

We all prayed.

The next morning there was an entirely new report about Shannon's prognosis. She not only made it through the night, but she was much improved. The doctors felt she would be all right.

Indeed she would. Shannon went on to be a college cheerleader and gymnast and received her Masters degree in early childhood development. There was not the least damage to her body or brain. This was my first experience with spiritual healing.

Interestingly enough, I didn't run out and investigate spiritual healing. I thought of it as an isolated experience and never dreamed that spiritual healing could apply to every day life or to me.

Many years after this experience, however, I did get interested in metaphysics. This eventually led me to the study of Christian Science healing. I recall my first two healings. The first one was with the help of a professional Christian Science healer and the second healing was alone, through my own prayer.

First of all, I was a smoker. I smoked at least two packages of cigarettes a day and more on weekends.

I tried many times, in vain, to stop smoking, but was unable and felt resigned to the fact that I was a slave to nicotine. Then I met a Christian Science practitioner. She agreed to give me metaphysical treatments through prayer each day in order to heal my addiction. When I asked her if she thought I would be healed, she always answered that she thought I would be.

In the beginning of our work together, I explained that, in order for me to know whether a healing had really occurred, she could not require me to stop smoking once she began her prayers. I was convinced that I could not stop anyway. She agreed.

We spoke each week about the healing work she was offering me. This went on for a few weeks. I was still puffing like a chimney. And, at this point, I was feeling a little embarrassed for her since I knew she was trying her best to heal me but, obviously, not succeeding (in my mind).

Then one day, she suggested we meet. In our visit, she told me ways she was being divinely led to work for me, based on her prayers. She said that she clearly saw that I was spiritually whole and complete without any need to impress others. She explained that she saw my spiritual identity free of the need to express sophistication in order to fit in socially or to receive love.

Frankly, I thought she was way off. I certainly was not aware of doing these things. I felt socially confident. Didn't she understand that it was a physical, not a social or emotional, problem?

Before I left, she asked me to participate in the healing. I agreed. She suggested that, each time I wanted to light a cigarette, to first pause and think of a synonym for God. And, in selecting a synonym, she asked that I think a truth about that synonym. I agreed, but told her that I felt unqualified to do the assignment.

She took me through it slowly. I thought of various synonyms (God is Love, Truth, Mind, etc.) and a simple truth about each of these. (i.e. Truth sets me free, Love meets all my needs, Mind knows what to do.) She verified my correctness. I was surprised that I got it right.

It sounded simple enough. I must admit that I had little faith that it would work. Nevertheless, on the way home, I lit up a cigarette and paused before doing so to think of a synonym for God, followed by a truth about the synonym.

I did this for the remainder of the afternoon. By early evening, I went to the table to pick up my pack of cigarettes and looked at them without any desire. I wondered. Could this be what she referred to as a spiritual healing?

The next morning again, I had no desire to smoke. By afternoon, I called her and told her what had happened and inquired if this was a healing and would it last?

She assured me that this was a spiritual healing and that it was permanent. She was right. My healing of nicotine addiction took place almost thirty years ago and I have not wanted or had a cigarette since. Total freedom from the addiction! It was amazing to me.

After this experience, I became vastly interested in spiritual healing. My primary interest was that, at last, I could connect with God. In fact, I was more interested in discovering Truth and connecting with God than I was interested in physical healing. To learn that connecting with God actually heals was even more engrossing.

I was beginning to see that every spiritual healing was proof of Love's presence and care. I was enthralled! It wasn't long after this healing that I discovered that I could heal myself through prayer. And it wasn't long after that that I discovered I could heal others through prayer. Prayer works.

My first healing through my own prayer

About a month after my healing of addiction to nicotine, I was visiting my mother-in-law, who was quite ill. During this time, I was making every effort to help her – doing the wash, bringing her things, tidying up, and cooking.

One afternoon, I decided to cook dinner with my mom's special recipe for pot roast. It was always a winner.

While the roast was cooking, I continued to do things to be helpful. However, I lost track of the time and I panicked once I realized that the roast had been in the oven too long. Without thinking, I ran to the kitchen, quickly opened the oven door, and started to pull out the roast with my bare hands.

Immediately I dropped the dish (thankfully, nothing spilled) and pulled back in horror of what I had done.

Standing in the middle of the kitchen, I looked at my red hands, experiencing enormous pain. The palms of my hands were burned and hurting. Blisters were already forming. I considered reaching for butter or ice, which is something I had done in the past for kitchen burns.

Just then it dawned on me to pray. But how? Not knowing exactly what I was doing, I opened my thought to God. I mentally asked for help. I used no words and was very brief.

Right away it occurred to me that God's angels were able to operate through me even though I didn't know how. I felt that Love was giving me whatever I needed.

There was nothing strange or mysterious about standing in the middle of the kitchen in the afternoon with burned hands and praying, waiting for a healing. The heavens didn't open up and I didn't see any angels or have any lightening bolt strike.

However, the burning in my hands ceased instantly. I stood there looking at them. I couldn't believe what had happened. I felt that the invisible God of Love had heard my prayer and answered me with healing.

The pain never returned. The redness began fading and by the next afternoon, the blisters were flat and rapidly disappearing. The problem ceased from the moment I prayed.

This spoke volumes to me. I had never prayed for myself for a spiritual healing before, and here, on the first time, I found the presence of Love with me and never knew it before. I saw that I have a relationship with a caring, loving Presence that I could access anytime. What a discovery!

Since that time, I have had personal healings too numerous to list and have been a part of thousands of other healings with others. I can tell you that prayer works. I can't think of anything more thrilling, can you?

The most important relationship of your life

The most important relationship of your life is with Love. Ask yourself: How do you characterize your present relationship with Love? Do you feel separate? Close? At one?

If you feel separate from God, you may feel that God is far off. You may not think to contact God because of the work involved (or you think it is work). You may be convinced that you don't know how to pray, have never quite understood if what you were listening to was God or yourself, and feel uncomfortable trying to pray since you have little faith in being successful. That's okay, keep trying and you will succeed. I promise.

If you feel close to God, you are listening throughout the day or at many intervals. God is prominent in your day and you feel you are being led by God. You will have a sense of stability and peace, even in hard times, since you know that you understand how to stay in touch with God and listen.

If you are at one with God, you are flowing in continual communion, tuned in, filled with desire to stay in touch, and wanting more. You will often know in advance of events what to anticipate and how to respond. You will have a strong feeling from people who suffer, beyond what they themselves know, since you and God are one, and you will know the way to help heal them.

The only way to learn how to ride a horse is to get on its back and experience the horse as you ride it.

The only way to learn to play a piano is to sit in front of the keys and practice playing them over and over.

And the only way to learn about God is to spend time with God – open, willing, and listening. Practice your relationship with God. This is how you strengthen your relationship.

When you love someone, you want to spend time with them, get to know them, and enjoy loving, sharing, and learning from them. This is the way we establish great relationships. Our relationship with Love is the same.

Your healing ability will improve as you work a little each day at it, through prayer.

The difference between prayer and meditation

You can, in fact, use many of the same meditative skills for prayer. Perhaps the biggest difference between meditation and prayer is that, in prayer, you are specifically acknowledging and connecting with Spirit. And, in prayer, you are reminding yourself where you place your faith. You are ready to connect with a loving Presence that you want to interact with. It is more than merely stilling the mind, though that is important in prayer as well.

We pray to God in love, service, devotion, faith, and worship. We pray to God for guidance, understanding, and healing.

In prayer, you are specifically listening to Love's angels to reveal their messages through your spiritual intuition. The healing effect may be a particular message or a spiritual sense or feeling.

When prayer works

Prayer works if you are sincere in your love for God – more interested in learning about the nature of God than in the outcome of what you most need.

I never beg, plead, or promise, "God, I'll do something for you, if You will only do this one thing for me." Prayer is not about manipulating God. It is not a gimmick to get what you want.

Spiritual healing is a sacred event. It involves sincere love for and interest in knowing God. Love for God isn't a bargaining chip. Yes, you can expect healings for your child, your job, your marriage, your financial problems, your health, and more. In fact, you can have healings everywhere in your life. Healings, however, usually don't come in a package with the answer you may outline or seek. Healings often come in a surprising way, and far better than you yourself could have arranged.

My least favorite mode of healing is when someone calls me and gives me what feels like an order for a healing. It makes me feel like a prayer grinder or a Santa Claus. It rarely happens anymore because I no longer indulge it and, instead, I encourage others to participate in their healing with me.

To learn how healing works, we need an attitude of humility and openness.

What obstructs healing is the pressure to by-pass our love for God and our need for divine guidance, and to go straight for results, which is actually not straight to the healing at all. It is straight away from God, while thinking you are praying.

First of all, exercise your right to take a moment and truly love God. Let your heart open wide to God. Stay in this wonderful place and experience the joy of your open heart pouring out love to God.

If you are praying in order to tell Love your problems, this is unnecessary. The all-knowing already knows. If you're praying to instruct the all-knowing, think again.

If you are praying to get results (have Spirit perform for you), then you will miss the spiritual experience of prayer. You'll soon be leaving the sacred place, drifting into the land of outcome orientation, "I prayed, but nothing happened." Healing prayer stays in a place of listening and expectation, with Love at the center. This takes practice.

Don't be in a hurry. Bring out your beautiful patience and allow yourself to slowly become aware of what happens in prayer.

It is important not to push for outcome. Prayer is a time to love God, listen, re-align, come into a sacred place within, gain guidance and inspiration, be grateful, and remember who you are.

From the moment you start to pray, you are receiving divine guidance. If you are praying with sincerity, the healing outcome will follow – just as the wake always follows the boat.

In prayer, we most need to think about what we can do to align ourselves with Love, and not what Love can do to align Itself with us. The difference is vast and will determine the speed and success of your healing.

If our goal is to align ourselves with Love, then we will listen to Love to tell us how to do this. If we ourselves knew, we wouldn't be praying for Love to show us. Prayer is the recognition of your need for Love's guidance in healing.

Prayer can be very fast. You can accomplish the state of prayer – enormous love for and surrender to God – in less than one second. It's not about the time you spend or the words you say or the pleading you do.

Prayer is my favorite place and I return to it over and over and over, day and night. This is the most healing place that exists. It is practicing your relationship with God, and with God telling you how to do it.

Prayer leads to growth

In healing prayer, you expect to grow. In fact, growth is inevitable when you pray. Growth means change. If your prayers are working, you are learning, growing, and changing.

Growth and change aren't necessarily comfortable. Prayer can be unsettling, especially when we are undergoing vast changes needed for coming into conformity with healing.

I received a call from a woman who described her physical condition as frightening. She had awakened that morning to find she was covered in spots. She asked me to pray and readied herself to go to the hospital emergency room.

Her main concern was to discover if she was contagious since she lived in a house with others and wanted to be protective to all. The doctor confirmed that it was a contagious virus.

When she called me after returning home from the emergency room, I had a different sense of it. My inner diagnosis, gained through prayer, was that she had been rapidly growing in her spirituality and something new was struggling to emerge within her. But something in her was not quite able to release and let go in order to fully move forward.

I felt in my gut that this was what we were really healing, though it appeared in the form of a virus. To my sense, it was more clearly a chemicalization she was experiencing, as in alchemy, when impurities fall away as the heat is increased. In this case, her growing spirituality was the heat. We continued to pray, though she felt doubtful about my intuition.

The third day of our prayers, she received the same insight that I had. She shared her inner life's self-doubts and lack of confidence and explained to me that, even as she described herself in this way, she could see that it no longer applied to her new, evolving self. She had come face to face with a position outgrown. To a healer, this is a sign of healing.

Inside of me, the angels were striking up their band to have a parade. I felt we had cleared the problem through our prayers and the answers were clear. That call was the turning point of the healing and the healing came forth the next day.

Prayer is communion with Love

Prayer is time spent with God or Love. It is communing in order to learn, be guided, experience, be informed, and influenced by the divine.

It is trusting that, by turning to something higher for help, something wonderful will occur that you yourself could not have thought of or created.

When I pray and ask for guidance, I absolutely love listening to see how God will guide me. I am fascinated to see that guidance always, and without exception, occurs.

It is not the words. It is the open heart and longing that moves us to a healing place. That is your measuring stick for effective prayer. Let your love for Spirit move you to the healing.

Prayer is deep listening

When I pray, I do a lot of listening. My prayers consist of turning to Love for answers. I never even think of telling Love what my problem is. I hear people describe their prayer as telling God things they feel God doesn't know. Are they kidding? Prayer is listening. Without listening, why would you pray?

In prayer, I am reminded of my spiritual origin. I recall my (and others) true nature as divine. I become calm and comforted. I am ready to awaken to a new view of things. I am aware that I am not alone. I am ready for new perspectives. I am ready to listen,

listen, listen – and know exactly how God is guiding me at that moment.

Healing is about renewal, regeneration, and growth. These are the things that a listening prayer produces.

Listening brings you into greater alignment with healing Love.

What happens in a prayer

You can pray anywhere. There are times I have excused myself from a social gathering to retreat to the ladies' room in order to close the stall door and pray.

During healing practice calls, I usually pray while someone is talking to me. I am listening to the caller to understand what he or she wants me to know. And I am also turning to Love to hear what I am being guided to see, know, say, or do. It works. The connection is always there.

When I am praying for myself, I am in a holding pattern of quiet stillness while turning to Love. Holding the space open for Love's healing influence, I allow the inner chatter to subside and become silent. I am aware that Love's healing presence is stilling the fears that I brought into the prayer.

When thoughts of criticism, doubt, judgment, opposition, fear, and disturbance come to your thought, let them go, like clouds floating by. Do not attach to these thoughts. They are not yours. You are moving into prayer in order to drop the load and to allow yourself to be separated from the problems. Something needs to be surrendered.

Release thoughts such as: "This prayer is not working. I still have the problem. Will I be healed? How will I be healed? What if I am not healed?" Recognize that these thoughts do not belong to your divine consciousness, created by God. Whenever you are aware of such thinking, just realize that you are leaving those thoughts and allowing the divine to lift you higher.

Facing our fears

Often when we sit down to pray, we are, for the first time, facing the fears we have been walking around with for awhile and ignoring. The beginning of prayer can sometimes be uncomfortable. It takes courage to stop ignoring fear and to create a new response to what most bothers you. That's okay, you have all the courage you need to pray and face whatever you most need to face in order to be healed. Remember, you are not alone. You are not going to God to see if God is there. God is already waiting.

At a time when we most need to pray, negativity can feel overwhelming. Please don't wait for the negativity to subside before you pray. Prayer, in fact, will aid enormously in removing or transforming the negativity. That is the very moment you most need to pray, in response to the negativity. This is a prime healing moment. At such times, pray with your focus on loving, connecting, and listening to Love as you allow the negativity to subside.

The energy of your prayer is completely opposite to the energy of the negative thoughts. Your positive, spiritual healing efforts are opposing all negativity. As more of Spirit comes through, you are, perhaps even unconsciously, neutralizing fears. Stand in the place of faith. Stand in your beautiful Light. Let the fears go.

As you release the negative thoughts, focus on listening. See what message Love has for you. The divine message is with you, unfolding even before you ask.

Allow the divine Presence to come forward and be active in your consciousness. Leave the world of appearances and doubts about healing. Remind yourself of your love for Spirit. Be renewed, restored, informed, and inspired. Listen with hunger and eagerness to know what is unfolding to you. Remember, you want to know what Spirit is telling you.

Believe it or not, you are building a case for your healing to unfold as you listen so sweetly for Love's healing message.

Let's pray together

Let's move now through a complete prayer session together so you can experience what takes place in my heart as I pray.

Find a comfortable place and provide yourself with a period of time without interruption. Decide how long you want to pray.

You may want to begin by reading a simple Truth such as a verse from the Bible, the Koran, the Torah, the Bhagavad Gita, Patanjali's Yoga Sutras, Buddhist teachings, a Course in Miracles, or the writings of Mary Baker Eddy, Joel Goldsmith, Ernest Holmes, Charles Fillmore, Paramahansa Yogananda, or any other deeply spiritual work where it is so condensed that you could open a page and find Truth active at a profound depth. Ask Love to lead you towards an anchoring, healing thought for your day, for greater understanding, and to guide your inspirational work.

For prayer of healing, before you pray, it may be helpful to identify what you intend to heal. You may even want to write it down and keep it in front of you if you need to remember.

Or you may wish to simply start your prayer in direct communion with Love.

As you sit comfortably, begin to relax. Release all tensions, anxieties, frustrations, and negative feelings as you relax into this golden moment with Love.

Allow your entire body to drop into deep relaxation. Move into stillness and quietness.

Open yourself to the divine Presence. Allow yourself to sense that divine Love is with you now. Breathe deeply into the fullness of this present moment and allow Love's presence to become more real to you. Receive it.

Open your heart with gratitude that you are in this wonderful Love presence that is caring for you and blessing you immeasurably at this and every moment.

Let Love's healing presence calm you. Feel the calm. Allow it to fill you with comfort. Acknowledge that you are filled with Love's comfort since you are of Love. Affirm that every thought from Love is a comforting thought.

Feel the peace. Sit in this Love space for a few moments as it sinks in deeply with Its message and touches you.

Realize how deeply you have longed for this Love. Accept Love's full presence with you now. You are no longer alone. You never were alone.

Divine Love has great hopes and desires for you which It intends to fulfill as you surrender to Love. In fact, Love is already fulfilled and your prayer is a time of awakening to this state as your very own state of being.

By coming into alignment with Love, your life changes. This is the way of healing. This wonderful Love presence causes you to remember your sacred identity as divine and holy. Your origin is divine. You are good, not bad.

This sacred Love presence pours out massive comfort, peace, rest, safety, and healing for you. Allow yourself to feel this great sense of comfort and healing. Know and feel deeply that you are safe, comforted, peaceful, harmonious, rested, joyful, abundantly supplied, supported, loved, deserving, adored, cherished, strong, able, immortal, and healed by Love.

Come even closer to Love

Come even closer to Love. The closer you come, the more you will feel Love's power. Humble yourself before this all powerful healing Presence. Be aware that Love's desire for you is happiness, wholeness, and wellness. Love wants nothing less for you than total blessing. It is always Love's intention to have you joyful and free, fulfilled and abundant, comforted and empowered. Love holds back nothing from you. Love wants you to have all good and to fill you with all good at this moment and every moment.

Know that, as you come closer to Love, it will change you. Allow Love to do its healing work within you. Place all your desires, attitudes, thoughts, understandings, perceptions, and actions in Love's capable, healing hands. Let Love slowly move on all these aspects of your being. Let Love alter the way you look at yourself at this moment.

Let Love lift you to higher thoughts and inform you of new things. Allow Love to lead you to new decisions that are better. Welcome all Love's changes.

Allow yourself to let in more of Love's massive comfort. Remain quiet. Notice your inner peace. It is within you now. Stay in this moment.

Become aware of your spirituality. This is a spiritual moment. Love your spirituality with honoring and cherishing. You are precious. The only self you are is a treasure to the entire universe. Release all that is not honoring of yourself. Release fears, doubts, worries, comparisons, nervousness, and all negative feelings, thoughts, and images. Release their recycling. Let them go now.

Thank Love for being with you and lifting you higher. Even if you don't yet feel lifted, you are in the presence of that which uplifts.

If there is anything troubling you, address this now. Ask Love to be fully present to counter your biggest concerns. Ask Love for positive, spiritual thoughts to help you. Ask for Love's influence and direction for doing this. Write down these powerful thoughts. Turn them into affirmations for your day's use. Pause now to listen and write.

Allow this loving presence to fill your own presence as you release all fears. Be willing to let them go – fears in the past, present, and future. Sitting in the divine Presence, realize that there is nothing to fear. In fact, there is no fear in Love's healing presence. Allow yourself to experience Love's complete freedom of all fear. Notice that you are outside of fear and that Love, instead of fear, is with you.

Allow yourself to feel the immense comfort, peace, encouragement, and assurance that is pouring forth to you from Love.

Listen to Love's angel thoughts

If there is something that you would like to focus on taking higher – such as your life purpose, a relationship, supply, health, age, outlook, emotions, a conflict, inner disturbance, or any other need – ask Love for specific guidance on this. Pause and listen.

Acknowledge that there may be something you may need to change, even in this very moment. Allow Love to tell you so you may experience Love's wonderful plan for you. Know that Love is gently and sweetly helping you.

Allow your attitudes to be adjusted by Love. Let Love touch your thoughts and lift them, bringing in more light of understanding where you most need it. Let Love teach you better ways that will free you, unchain you, and lift you from burden, fear, and suffering. Stay open to Love. Feel Love's healing comfort.

In Love's healing presence, angels are with you – by the gazillion! Listen to them. They are divine messages from Love. What are they saying to you? Intuit their messages.

Love's presence unfolds precious healing messages for you every moment. They may come in the form of a mental picture or image, a word, or a sensing. You may want to take a note of what is coming through right now and read it later as it guides you through the day.

Ask Love for:

- healing
- divine influence
- guidance
- direction
- understanding
- protection

If you need to be loved and appreciated, ask Love to guide you in creating the perfect relationships for you. Ask Love how to do this. Ask to receive the opportunities for sharing and closeness with those who are waiting to bless you and whom you will be led to also equally bless.

Ask Love to lead you to those who are appointed to love you generously and who also wait for your generous love. Ask Love to pour forth all blessings of loving experiences so that your life may be abundant with Love all day and evening.

Remember, let Love guide you. Do not guide Love.

If you need life purpose healing, ask Love to reveal your mission to you in a way that is perfectly clear. Your age is inconsequential. Wait to receive Love's messages, each one filled with healing inspiration, enlightenment, and power to inform you.

Expect your mission to be eternal, infinite, and godly. Expect your mission to be spiritual. Do not necessarily expect your mission to be an occupation. What is Love telling you is the next step for your progress?

Now take a couple of minutes in comp
stillness and silence to let Love speak to you direct
Pause. Write down what Love communicates to you.

Surrender in humility

Your beautiful gratitude causes you to be in a place of wonderful surrender. Surrender further as you allow humility to bring you into even greater divine alignment. Consciously let go of false defenses of anger, ego, and pride. These invaders are not part of you. You are Love's flowering beauty of openness and surrender. In your divine selfhood, you and Love coexist as One. You are divine Love's healing presence.

Humility is fully operating within you and it means that you are willing to come more fully into conformity with Love's divine nature, your own true nature and identity.

Come to Love with an open mind ready to be filled. Ask the Presence of All-Knowing Love to inform you of every thing you need to know.

Let Love loose in your consciousness. Let Love re-arrange your entire system of thinking about the problem you are healing or the guidance you are seeking. Let the divine overtake you to bring forth healing.

Let Love bring forward divine thoughts, awareness, and experiences that need to come to the forefront.

Give Love permission to rearrange your entire consciousness – your thoughts, outlooks, desires, understandings, and attitudes. Allow yourself to be inconvenienced and even uncomfortable as you allow yourself to come into Love alignment.

Realize that, even in the darkest recesses of your consciousness, Love is there, filling you with healing light.

ught to forgiveness. It is time now
the burden of guilt – all of it. Allow
be forgiven. Realize that you are on a
curve for this entire human experience.
yourself to learn from all mistakes – past,
ent and future. Let them go now in forgiveness
or yourself. Ask yourself, "What have I learned from
my mistakes?" Celebrate your learning.

If there are any who have been harmed by your
learning, pray now that this may be divinely
corrected and that they may be in a place of blessing
from this experience so they, too, may go higher.

Take a moment to also forgive all those who have
wronged you. Release old hurts and pains and
discomfort from people's actions. Let go of grudges,
resentments, blame, condemnation, and all anger.
Release words spoken and unspoken that you
associate with hurtful times. The light within you is
shining more brightly as you release these misgivings
for all time. Do this now.

Forgiveness is vital to your oneness with Love. It
is impossible to be in oneness with Love and not
forgive. Forgiveness does not mean that you are
condoning what was done wrongly to you.
Forgiveness also does not mean that the door is then
wide open for the person, or persons, to repeat the
offense.

Forgiveness simply means that your heart is
clean, pure, and filled with peace, allowing Love to
reside with you. Nothing takes precedence over
Love's and your oneness.

Grow in wisdom

Ask that Love take you into its healing wisdom to
reveal to you anything hidden from your senses.

Ask Love, "What am I learning in my life right now?" Listen for Love's answer and consciously claim it as your own. Ask Love, "What am I ignoring that most needs healing?" (Often I even ask Love what to ask.) Then listen. Accept loving guidance from Wisdom now.

Be willing to let go of any and all resistance to what is being called forth in you for healing or for your greatest blessing today.

Look deeply into your relationships. If there is any sense of unfairness, discord, inequality, stress, fear, unhappiness, or abuse, pray about this now. Ask how you may be an instrument of bringing forth healing change.

Be open to making new and wiser decisions. Be willing to have Love's courage to lovingly speak up if there is something that is calling you forth to be said or done. Be willing to gracefully end a relationship, if necessary. Ask that you may be guided to act in Love's wisdom in all these matters.

Trust Love

Trust Love to answer your prayer, bless your life, and bring you all good.

People who were raised by parents or guardians that either neglected or abused them find trust very difficult. I certainly can understand why. However, without trust in good, your life will never leave the stage of insecurity, stress, depression, and overwhelm. Do you really plan to continue to live this way?

Willingness to open to the idea of trusting good will slowly teach you how to do this. Your happiness depends on it. Begin now.

Whatever the day brings forth, or the days ahead bring forth, you and Love are meeting each moment together with divine instruction. Trust Love to be with you every moment, all day and night, and to enable you to rise above all difficulty through Love's healing presence, inspiration, and wisdom.

Trust Love to shape and mold you in a clearer expression of the divine. Trust that you can stay awake to Love's guidance all through the day and evening, and follow it as best as you can. Nothing more is required of you.

Widen your prayer

Turn your thought to the world's sufferings. Ask Love to end all suffering on the planet – for individual hearts, families, businesses, nations, refugees, those in prisons, the starving, homeless, and hopeless, and those alone, hurting, crying, and in pain. Ask Love to end suffering to these precious ones to whom we send our love and affection.

Pray that they become aware that Love is in their hearts operating as a law of healing to all that concerns them. Pray that they be fed by Love, treated with love and compassion, receive loving care, and awaken to Love's guidance and mercy. Pray that their suffering may be healed today.

Let your love move to our global environment – precious animals, natural resources, our atmosphere, and all places of nature's beauty. Ask Love to send its healing presence to protect, enlighten, and preserve us.

Picture a column of light coming down to all the people and all the places on earth. See the light of Love coming down, blessing everyone and every place. See everyone covered in Love's protective light of healing. See everyone – including yourself and loved ones – safe in Love's embrace.

See yourself as a river of Love flowing out towards everyone, blanketing them in love. Even people who have wronged you are waiting for your healing love to reach them. Reach everyone now with your massive love.

See yourself asking Love's sacred questions all day, "How healed do you feel in my presence? How loved do you feel in my presence?" See yourself sharing your beautiful heart of love so that all feel deeply loved and blessed by you.

Acknowledge that everyone you meet today and all who you think about today will be for the purpose of expressing love to them. Love flows through you on this lovely day. This is Love's healing way.

Think of your loved ones, those closest to you. Ask that Love's blessings pour into their lives with healing. Know that Love is caring for them equally with the intention to bless them in all ways – in all their relationships, health, finances, their progress, protection, strength, ability, outlook, and joy.

Give gratitude

Thank Love for its healing presence and care.

Love doesn't need the thanks. This is for you to further open your heart to recognize and acknowledge the good.

Think about all the good in your life. See all this good coming from divine Love. Allow yourself to be filled with thanks for all your blessings.

Think of words adequate to describe your blessings. Words like wonderful, great, and marvelous.

Thank Love – in advance – for answering your prayer.

Allow the deep inner peace you now feel to stay with you all day. Expect the power of this deep inner peace to counter all frustrations, fears, worries, pressures, and stress. Allow these to subside. Feel Love's calming presence with you.

As you close your prayer:

- Thank Love for its healing presence and influence all during your prayer.

- Thank Love for staying with you and operating through you all day long today.
- Thank Love for causing you to be a blessing to everyone, including yourself, throughout your lovely day.

Open your heart wide to flow with thanks and love for this wonderful, healing prayer.

Throughout the day, use the empty moments to reconnect – while eating, dressing, walking, driving, and waiting. At these moments, breathe mindfully and smile. You may want to take moments to review your affirmations and what you journaled. These are good moments to tune in to Love's presence, acknowledging that you are never alone. Love is with you, always – loving, blessing, comforting, calming, assuring, guiding, and healing you.

Give Love enormous gratitude for being with you always and for being a constant, eternal, caring presence. Stay with this sense of Love's healing presence with you all day and evening. Know that this Presence is guiding you for the highest good throughout your life – in all your relationships, conversations, decisions, events, attitudes, and outcomes, for yourself and your loved ones. And while Love accompanies you each moment, you are awakening to Love's Allness everywhere at once.

If it is evening, let Love tuck you in tonight so that you may sleep with deep rest and peace, awakening refreshed and ready for another day with Love's healing presence. If you awaken in the night, feel Love's presence still with you. Keep the space open for you to know that Love is with you, always.

Such reverent prayer opens the door for us to move from false beliefs to spiritual wisdom.

Chapter 7

Moving from False Beliefs to Spiritual Wisdom

Knowledge changes what we believe to be true. What we once believed to be hard core fact is no longer perceived as true. Our knowledge is always changing.

Think back to the time when people believed the earth was flat. Suppose you lived then and someone told you that the earth was not flat, but round. This may have been an impossible leap of perceptual change for you. Yet, today, we think of that shift of perception as a baby step in understanding our planet. The key fact to remember here is that the earth never changed. Our perception changed. And our changing beliefs did not stop there.

The Einstein revolution in perception

Consider the new knowledge that Einstein introduced and the way it changed what we presently believe to be true. Until Einstein presented his theory of relativity, we believed that matter was solid mass. We believed exactly what our eyes saw.

Then he proved that what appeared to be solid mass was actually energy, swirling molecules, and not at all solid. What a change of perception that was!

I keep this in mind when healing physical problems. Listening to symptoms of an illness, dysfunction, injury, or disease, I replace these descriptions with images of the true person, who is not a solid material mass at all. From there, it is an easy shift to perceive them energetically as thought, spiritual, and perfect. In healing, all roads lead back to Love and our identity as Love's own expression.

Quantum physicists go even further than Einstein

Since Einstein's time, quantum physicists have changed our beliefs even more radically. They have won the Nobel Prize showing that the lowest common denominator of a particle reveals that the particle ceases being material. Matter, then, is viewed as a law of probabilities. And this law of probabilities has properties of self-renewal, regeneration, and self-perpetuation.

This sounds more like a description of immortality, not materiality, being the building block of our existence!

The next time you think of yourself with a physical problem, you can shift this perception and go past the swirling molecules and particles, and instead, see yourself as the substance of the divine law of Love – self-renewing, regenerating, and self-perpetuating. This is a very healing thought at a profound and powerful level.

Medical research proves that spiritual healing works

Larry Dossey, M.D., has authored many well researched books on the subject of mind/body and healing. His contribution, along with those of Dr.

Herbert Benson and Dr. Bernie Siegel, has been remarkable.

Dr. Dossey reports on a blind study research, meaning that the patients did not know the content of the experiment. They only knew that their bodies were being monitored at many physiological levels.

The experiment consisted of a healer stationed in one room and the patient in the other room. The patient did not know that the healer was present or engaged with thought or prayer for them. When the researcher "gave the word" to the healer, the healer did healing work, focusing on the patient. And when the researcher said to stop, the healer stopped doing his or her healing work.

This procedure was done randomly many times and with many healers of various religious and non-religious backgrounds. They also varied the patients. All were victims of severe illnesses.

The experiments were blind so that the placebo effect could be ruled out. If the patients knew someone was praying for them, it may have had an influence over them, causing them to believe the treatment was having a positive effect. There was, therefore, no expected outcome from the patients.

The study showed an overall influence of improved health when the healers were told to do their work. There were positive effects such as improved oxygen in the blood, less stress in the body shown by calmer brain wave patterns, and improved immunization.

We know for certain that we can change beliefs. We know for certain that our thoughts influence our state of being. We know for certain that prayer and spiritual healing have an effect on the body and mind.

Harvard's long term research on the mind/body relationship

When I attended one of Harvard's conferences on Spirituality and Healing in Medicine, I listened to Herb Benson, M.D. speak. He has spent over thirty years researching the mind/body connection for Harvard's Medical School and we owe him a great debt of gratitude. Dr. Benson feels that between sixty and ninety percent of all visits to the doctor's office are stress related. Stress and anxiety and fear are causal to health conditions. Experts like Benson are cheerleaders for meditation, which they consider to be great preventive care for good health.

Their research has been monumental in proving the connection between the mind and body.

Bernie Siegel, M.D. enlists the aid of his patients during surgery

Dr. Siegel, best-selling author of books on healing and a tireless advocate of the healing potential within each of us, is another giant contributor in mind/body research. He writes of telling his anesthetized surgery patients how the operation is progressing. He may ask them to lower their heart rate, naming a specific number such as 86. And he watches the response as the unconscious patient proceeds to lower his or her heart rate to the specified number.

There are an abundant, available number of studies today proving that our thoughts have vast influence over our bodies. My entire healing practice is based on this. Spiritual healing is more than just the mind controlling or affecting the body. Spiritual healing is the influence of the Mind of God effecting the entire life of man.

Love's practical self care

Would Love ever neglect itself? Would Love fail to offer caring and intelligent attention to itself? Never. And neither would you as you practice your daily Love alignment.

For example, you already know that your body deserves and needs to experience relaxation, not stress – *every* day, and not *some* days. Your body needs healthy meals and reasonable exercise every day with plenty of drinking water as well as rest. These are needs that are not going to go away. They require our attention.

This, of course, also means that beliefs occur when you break nature's laws of self care. Beliefs of being run down create more beliefs of vulnerability to illness. The body operates at an optimum level when it is treated with respect.

Moderation and balance are always wise. Overeating and over exercise are just as poor treatment as under eating and no exercise. No matter your age, meeting your body's needs is essential to your good health and long life. Practicing balance in all these areas is a life long discipline.

Years of smoking and excessive alcohol or drugs, for example, take a toll. With practical caretaking, you can thank yourself for years to come. And your loved ones will thank you as well.

Just because you are living spiritually does not exempt you from the need to meet these basic needs. Real spirituality is grounded, wise, and loving, with generous and continuous self care. Love would have it no other way. If you need a visit with your care physician – whether a spiritual practitioner or a medical practitioner – by all means love yourself enough to receive all the help you need, and early on. You are far too precious to neglect.

The decision to seek medical help versus spiritual healing

It is my humble opinion that you need not necessarily quit going to the doctor simply because you have decided that you are now spiritual and you want to heal yourself spiritually. There is a great deal of study, learning, and proving involved in spiritual healing. To begin now is a wonderful idea, and you can do so using practical wisdom in your everyday self care.

There should never be guilt associated with healing. We need to be free of self judgment in all areas of healing, and free to make the right decisions, without pressure, and with great lovingkindness to ourselves.

I, myself, have not visited a doctor for almost thirty years. But I have considered consulting medical help from time to time, preparing myself to do so should a problem fail to yield. The spiritual ideas in this book, however, have guided me, my clients, and my family through many crises and offered complete, successful healings.

My suggestion to you is to begin by reading this book and other books on the subject of healing and learn through self-practice. Offer plenty of time and patience to educate yourself on this all important subject. And, by all means, take every practical step to take impeccable care of your health.

A decision not to see a doctor, based on the fact that you would rather not have medical help, is not really bringing God into the picture as a primary motive for healing. And it is not enough for healing.

Spiritual healing without Spirit does not work. You can expect to experience spiritual healing as you grow and apply the truths of this book, and certainly other books, too. As you gain more insight, you will learn better how to approach spiritual healing.

Perceiving reality from the Highest Self

Perception is everything in spiritual healing. As we know, there are many ways to look at the same event. Yet, which perception is true? More importantly, which perception is healing?

Your life is not determined by circumstances and conditions external to you. Your life is determined by what you tell yourself about what is occurring. It is not what happens to you that determines your experience. It is how you perceive it that most determines your experience.

When my daughter Kaia was a toddler, we were taking a walk around the block, and she started playfully running away from me. However, she tripped and fell, hitting her bottom lip on the hard pavement.

When I ran to pick her up, she was screaming and also bleeding. I was horrified that my child had cut her lip while only a couple feet away from me. I scooped her up in my arms and began running home as she cried.

I was only half a block away when I began to question myself. Why am I running? What is my plan to help her once I get to the house?

My thought went immediately to God and I slowed to walking, speaking to her in a calm tone as I held her. As I prayed, I thought of our happy day together that could not be separated from God, and, in fact, had been blessed by God. That was an angel thought. Then came more angels. I was moving from false beliefs to spiritual wisdom. My perception was changing.

I reasoned that Love's blessings added no curse, but continued to immerse us in its total blessing. I also thought of her as Love's expression, and I remembered her Highest Self identity. This small turning to Love only took seconds. But it was enough to immediately awaken me to remember who she was and to have her stop crying and for the bleeding to totally end.

When we arrived home, I saw that the cut on her lip was almost completely closed. That was the last of the injury. I had simply changed my perception, reaching for divine Love's healing help.

The understanding and use of metaphysics is helpful in healing. Meta means above – above the physical.

When your perceptions rise above what *appears* or *feels* to be real and you turn to divine Love, healing begins to take place. This occurs when you recall your divinity and spiritual origin.

Do you see that knowing and remembering your Highest Self is the basis for all spiritual healing? Who are you? This is the all determining question that will give you the healing information you need.

The choice I made between two views when Kaia was healed was simple. I could see Kaia as a helpless, vulnerable, small, young child who was injured. Or, I could view her as Love's Highest Self, inseparable, perfect, whole, indivisible, and incapable of falling away from Love, even for a moment. Only one of these views has the power to heal.

Are you a mortal with a problem? Or are you outside the problem, existing as Love's Highest Self in Love's condition and not in a problem?

The observer and observed are one

Quantum physicists have demonstrated that the perceiver and the perceived are one. What we are perceiving is influenced by what we *think* we see. How subjective our experience of reality!

If the observer *redefines* what is being observed, and defines it, instead, according to Love's higher law, then the perception will change according to

Love's healing law. This is proven every day in my healing practice.

Some spiritual perceptions take a great deal of repetitive work to bring about a healing.

This is a good place to remind ourselves that intellectual metaphysics, without Love, is not true spiritual healing.

If you rely on your own intellect rather than Spirit, you will feel like you are all alone, trying to heal yourself by your knowledge. To the extent that you edit out Love, you suffer and healing becomes burdensome.

As we continue to open up to a full discussion on the nature of beliefs, please be open to think of yourself as from a divine Source, and from Love. Please feel the living, caring presence of Love guiding you every moment and in every way, including your thoughts.

Sometimes metaphysics is so filled with knowledge that it seems that we are trying to master a body of knowledge to heal ourselves. Nothing could be further from reality. Healing needs to come from the heart and soul, as well as the mind. Let the spirit of Love move through all your logic. You have seen how quickly and easily some of my healings have been.

While we look at beliefs and changing perceptions of reality, we always remember that Love creates all that truly exists. It is primarily Love, and not intellect, guiding your healings and informing you what to believe or accept as true. Love, and not you, is in the driver's seat of every spiritual healing.

Sometimes we can be so engrossed in the intellectual aspect of healing that we can lose sight of the all-important and only true healer, Love. Love takes the weight off your shoulders to be responsible for figuring things out. We can not do this alone. We need Love to show us the way while we actively express discernment between what is true and what is belief.

Are we to fear false beliefs?

It is important to keep in mind that, at no time, does a belief have power to harm or hurt you, unless you believe it. Remember when people believed the earth was flat. Did this belief have real power over them?

It was pure ignorance and they suffered from this limitation until the belief was no longer believed.

Never fear a false belief. What's to fear? If we add two plus two and get five, do we need to be afraid? No, we merely need to correct the mistake. But, as long as we believe that five is the correct answer, it will affect all our other mathematical calculations.

False beliefs are false conclusions. They *appear* to be true and that is why we believe them. All false beliefs are illusions.

There are certain truths in spiritual healing. One is, if something appears to be true, yet it is unlike Love, then it is a false belief. You need to keep working to awaken from the false assumption of a belief, while being guided by Love until you no longer believe the belief. The result is healing. We are always working to remove all blocks to healing and experience our Highest Self.

We suffer from false beliefs

We do not suffer from something that is real. We suffer from the *belief* that something is real. It is an indication that we are not viewing Love as all present.

False beliefs do not indicate what is true or real, but only what appears to be true or real. We tend to believe all that we see, hear, touch, taste, and smell.

Generally, our beliefs come from these material senses.

When suffering from any belief, we can do a great deal to awaken. We can remind ourselves that, in Truth, we are derived from Love. Love is who we are. We can stay awake to this. Love causes us to awaken from the dream of a belief. It is helpful to remind ourselves that, as Love's awakened being, we cannot be deceived by beliefs appearing as truth.

Love is with you always to offer you the light of healing and to cause you to understand the true nature of all reality as Love.

Instruction on perception from the master healer, Jesus

Here is a remarkable account from John, the beloved disciple of Jesus, about Jesus' suffering on the cross.

A friend copied this down from the scraps of St. John's memoirs when they were displayed at the British Museum. Here is what I learned.

John was with Jesus at the cross, overwhelmed by his perception of Jesus' suffering. He fled to the Garden of Gethsemane where they had prayed together earlier. John writes:

I, John, when I saw him suffer did not even abide his suffering but fled unto the Mount of Olives. And my lord, Jesus, standing in the midst of the garden and enlightening it, said, 'John, unto the multitude below in Jerusalem, I am being crucified. But I am here and unto thee I speak.'

These are two contradictory, yet astounding accounts, of the same event. Which, do you think, was true? The perception of Jesus on the cross? Or the perception of Jesus who simultaneously appeared to John in a place a good distance away?

Let's review this slowly. At the Garden of Gethsemane, Jesus offered John a new perception of himself. Rather than viewing and pitying Jesus as dying on a cross, Jesus showed John that he was in a state of enlightenment, and not suffering.

This is a 2,000 year old instruction on perception from a Master Healer who gained this instruction from his Highest Self, Love. Jesus instructed John to review again what he thought was true about what was occurring to Jesus, and to reconsider his perception. Was Jesus suffering? Or was he separate from suffering, in a state of enlightenment?

Let's apply this to you. Take a moment and identify your number one problem. Now re-frame it where you are now viewing yourself outside the problem and in a state of enlightenment. You are spiritual. Gently hold this lovely, healing view while you allow your condition to rearrange itself around your Highest Self's perception.

As Einstein said, "Problems cannot be solved at the same level of awareness that created them."

In order to heal a problem, you must go outside the problem and re-view it from a higher perspective gained from divine Love.

Love then will out-picture an improved state of being, more in conformity with Truth. And in proportion to your doing this steadfastly, you will realize healing. This is the healing law of Love. It reveals your true identity as divine. Why does this method work? Because a false belief is not based on reality and Truth reveals this.

An observer observes with non-attachment

Here is the best way to shift a perception towards healing. First, we need to acquire a healthy detachment from the events and circumstances of our lives and assume the role of an observer – especially in problem areas.

For example, think of yourself lying down on the ground, looking up at the sky, watching the clouds go by. As each cloud moves before you, it represents a thought or perception. You are an observer.

As you lie there, you can objectively watch the clouds, one by one, and think, "This is an interesting one," or, "I really like this one." But you do not say, "This cloud is me."

As you continue to lie there watching the clouds or thoughts, while remaining detached, you see dark clouds rolling by. You then say, "This one is a dark cloud." Again, you would not say, "This dark cloud is me and represents my life at this point. This cloud's color, moisture content, velocity, mass, and activity are me. I cannot stop the inevitable rain that I will produce. Therefore, I am having a bad day."

You would have no such confusion.

Instead, when you see a cloud, or thought that is dark and foreboding, you can be an observer and let it go by saying, "This is not me."

The process of using both logic and asking Love is how we distinguish Love's reality from beliefs. And it is all important in spiritual healing.

I propose to you that, if you will take this attitude towards your darkest problems and detach yourself from them while you also look at a higher perception of yourself based on Love, you will experience healing.

The place of non-attachment is a place of learning. It is a place where we observe and reflect, contemplate and listen.

Remember who you are. Remember also who you are *not*.

Don't be confused by thoughts. Just because you have a thought does not mean that the thought is true or real. Thought is changeable and so are its manifestations.

We are bombarded by thousands of thoughts every single day. You can be the determiner of your state of being as you exchange your thoughts with the thoughts and perceptions of your Highest Self.

It appears that you are the creator of your reality. But actually you are the perceiver of Love's ongoing reality. By perceiving as Love, you unite with Love. The result is spiritual healing.

Healing is more than a mental exercise. It is a spiritual perception guided by Love to replace a false perception. The only real question is, "Are you listening to Love's wisdom?"

Repetition of treatment is important

Although many healings are immediate, generally, the deeper healings do not take place overnight. Yet these are my favorite because they are so life enhancing.

Deeper healings involve learning, intuition, attitude change, perception change, willingness, determination, and generous love and patience with yourself and others. This generally requires repeated prayer and treatment.

For example, if you have had a lifetime of guilt, and you develop a physical problem, do not be surprised that this may be the time you will need to learn to practice self-forgiveness in order to change your habit of guilt. You may further need to increase your defense system, speak up, become more visible to yourself, love yourself more, discover your guiltlessness, and learn to take an unwavering stand for your innocence.

Also, if you have had a life time of anger, and you develop a physical problem, do not be surprised if this will be the time you will need to address the problem of anger. In healing such a case, you will need to learn a new response other than anger.

Your success in healing will depend on how much you persevere and actually change your habits. This means, of course, that habits of accusation, blame, condemnation, or hate will need to go. And instead, they will need to be exchanged with the opposite response. So you will be learning to respond with behavior that is harmonious, peaceful, and mild. Since anger is toxic to others, it is equally toxic to the person who repeatedly feels or expresses it.

Most of us are not aware of our behavior, since we are accustomed to it. Healing brings up all these things for us and, once cleared, causes us to have greater overall freedom and happiness.

As Light workers in the field of healing, we cannot afford to be naïve about how healing comes about. I hope that this book is an education for you in that respect.

Repetition is the life of a healer. Reminding yourself repeatedly of the infinite, true view and the real perception of yourself and others, based on Love's reality, and following up with permanent changes in behavior is the way of spiritual healing. Most healings are based on repetition – repeated prayers, repeated treatments, repeated watchfulness, and repeated learning from Love's fresh inspiration. This is the way that awakening occurs, and hidden habits – which were before invisible – now become visible to you and you can then change them.

How long do you work on a spiritual healing? As long as it takes. When should you give up? Never. Why? Because Love is at work right now, bringing forth healing in your very being.

Examples of moving from false perceptions to spiritual wisdom

Until false perceptions are replaced, we do not experience the freedom of healing. For example, the perception that "Someone is my enemy" creates the false belief of separation from Love. This perception is not based on your Highest Self.

People call me complaining about the way their friends and loved ones treat them and I sometimes wonder why they are referring to them as their friends and loved ones. Have they read a definition of enemy lately?

I must also say that, often, the most loving people don't even complain when they are treated poorly. They actually assume that they, themselves, must have done something wrong to deserve such poor treatment! It's time for a spiritual wake up call. Is it any wonder what needs to be healed here?

To begin to heal this, identify what the person is doing that creates suffering for you. Be willing to name it to yourself as harmful behavior. Realize that because of this repeated harmful behavior, you may need to take strong action to protect yourself. This may mean you will need to speak up to have it changed. This may even mean ending the relationship.

This all important work is a first step in healings that come from toxic relationships. Please do not skip over this step. If this is what you are suffering from, it is the step you have avoided for so long that you now are faced with the absolute necessity of healing it. This means facing the music and now. Once this has begun, you can then go to the next step of healing your perception of them.

In considering your perception of the person who is causing you suffering, begin to allow your perception of him or her to go higher.

I am not suggesting you place yourself in harm's way or make them your best friend or even that you stay in a relationship with them. I am merely speaking here of the healing work of changing your thought to re-label this person as Love's Highest Self. Why? Because, whether or not you stay in the relationship, you will still carry around the *thought* of them in your consciousness. If you are carrying around the thought of a disturbed relationship, it will need to be healed. I have seen people spend an entire lifetime carrying around an unhealed resentment or hurt while the party who caused it was not even seen for decades.

Claim inner peace and oneness with Love right where you perceive there is a problem, either with them or yourself. By offering exchanges, exchanging a false perception for Love's true perception, you can slowly, or quickly, change the outcome in order to have peace within. Actually, in truth, you are not changing reality, though it may appear so as you are healed. You are, instead, waking up to reality.

Consider how often our perception is opposing our Highest Self. For example, when someone rejects us, we tend to think, "I am not loved and I am hurt." This perception, if left unopposed, may create the false belief that "I am not worthy or valuable or important enough to receive love." Nothing could be further from the truth! Yet our lives consist of the out-picturing of these beliefs. As long as we believe beliefs, we manifest their outcomes.

We can, instead, listen to the inner voice of our Highest Self and state "I am worthy, valuable, and important to the entire oneness of all being. My presence is a necessity to all success. My purpose is indispensable to the collective whole." Needless to say, thinking this one time will be helpful, but most likely will not bring about a new pattern or permanent healing. We have old tapes to erase. New tapes, based on our identity as divine, need to be firmly established until the old tapes no longer play in our minds. This does not happen overnight.

Another common perception is about our bodies. The thought, "I have a physical problem" is created by the false belief that "I am vulnerable and subject to conditions outside my control."

If you weigh this negative thought against the perception of the Highest Self, however, you will not agree at all with the view of yourself having a physical problem with a condition of vulnerability. Rather than measuring how you are by how you feel, measure how you are based on how Love is. This will create a higher perception that will heal you, sending a new message throughout your system.

Every day, I receive calls reporting perceptions of physical problems. Yet, in addressing them, I do not take them in. Remaining objective, I put it through my spiritual sieve, and re-view it. I hardly realize I am re-viewing it, since I mostly stay in Love's reality all the time.

Making exchanges of a material perception for a spiritual and true perception of a person, I remind myself of his or her true state of divinity. I become the perceiver who perceives divine reality. The perceiver and the perceived become one. This heals.

I may, for example, remind myself that this person is spiritual, perfect, and invulnerable. I may mentally expand on this theme for a while.

Sometimes it takes repeated treatments. But each treatment awakens me to an even clearer sense of the truth regarding a case, until the truth has sufficiently awakened my thought and I am clear that Truth, and not the problem, is supreme and real. This is the way spiritual healing works. I find this fascinating, don't you?

Energy follows thought

If you don't like what you are manifesting in your life, begin to examine the thoughts or images that you are recycling. Don't let them re-define you away from your Highest Self. Challenge yourself to oppose these thoughts or mental images and take them higher to a spiritual basis.

As we embody Love's oneness, we utilize mental energy which creates new thought patterns and therefore new, improved manifestations. Matter is merely a derivative of thought.

Buddhists practice the importance of watching their habits. They feel that when the thought patterns are negative, it creates bad habit energy, which eventually manifests negatively in life. They are correct.

What are false beliefs?

Below, are some common false beliefs. As you review the list, think of how these beliefs tend to redefine you. Consider, however, that a belief does not truly identify who you are. It is necessary to challenge beliefs. Think of the fact that when you believe any belief, you allow this to separate you from your true identity as Love's expression or your Highest Self.

Healing occurs by exchanging false beliefs for Love's reality. Beliefs are an opportunity to awaken to spiritual enlightenment. Begin to become aware of beliefs and detach from them, separating yourself from their illusive pull.

As you review some of the following beliefs, observe that they do not describe you or anyone else. Think like a healer.

Common false beliefs

The following tend to enter our thoughts as "I am..." and they subjectively seem to be true, but they are not. It is a false belief that you are:

- afraid
- ashamed
- unworthy
- anxious
- worried
- inadequate
- lonely
- isolated
- behind
- guilty
- ugly
- oppressed
- defenseless
- uninspired
- alone
- outnumbered

- excluded
- rejected
- nervous
- aging
- dull
- boring
- bored
- ignorant
- stressed
- tired
- grouchy
- impoverished
- angry
- imbalanced
- drained
- depleted
- depressed
- tense
- hated
- hating
- out of control
- prejudiced
- insecure
- unsupported
- abandoned
- unsure
- confused
- vulnerable
- unalert
- stuck
- stagnant
- jealous
- mediocre
- lazy
- unable
- alone
- wishing
- longing
- burdened
- labored
- struggling
- lacking
- losing
- ineffective
- dishonest
- damaged
- hurt
- criticized
- condemned
- unloved
- failing
- needy
- opposed
- pulled
- dominated
- subordinate
- critical
- proud
- defensive
- overly sensitive
- undeserving
- selfish
- uncomfortable
- resistant
- hopeless
- overwhelmed
- unfulfilled
- dissatisfied
- unclear
- lost
- confused
- indecisive
- small

- pretending
- unhappy
- victimized
- sad
- obsessive
- craving
- yearning
- addicted
- willful
- compulsive
- controlling
- stubborn
- suicidal
- bruised
- regretful
- miserable
- traumatized
- imbalanced
- frantic
- distrustful
- worsening
- stupid
- powerless

More false beliefs

Sometimes, we may think we are the victim of:
Unfairness, injustice, deception, hate, evil, apathy, neglect, harm, collision, betrayal, accident, partiality, prejudice, violence, coldness, cruelty, low self esteem, criticism, condemnation, blame, accusation, rejection, or abuse.

Superstition is also a false belief

We suffer greatly from hidden superstitions. For example, in response to misfortune, we often tell ourselves any number of things like:
- "I may deserve this. I may have done something wrong.
- I may be paying for bad things that I did recently, or from my past.
- I may be paying for my ancestors' wrong doing.
- Perhaps someone is hating me and wanting harm to come to me.
- I'm unlucky.

- I've had it so good lately that it's now time
  for something bad to happen. After all,
  things can't be good all the time!"

Another self-sabotaging superstition occurs when we feel our very happiest and we say to ourselves, "This is too good to be true. Something is probably around the corner to ruin this. I know it!"

It's no wonder why we are afraid of growing. Superstitious doom hangs over every stage of growth declaring "Growth is always painful! I'm having growing pains."

All of this is superstition. Don't give your power away to it. Rise above the false belief of ancient ignorance, uneducated guesses, and ridiculous guilt conditioning.

One day, we will look back on our present superstitions and see them to be as absurd as when our ancestors believed that God was angry when lightening struck or a volcano exploded. Our present superstitions are these same ancient beliefs only appearing in more subtle forms today. They represent the belief that we can continue to suffer from ignorance and self-fulfilling limitations. We can become aware of this now and question the superstitions we now accept as true.

It is not unreasonable to expect good all the time. When you live in oneness with Love, you experience powerful insight into healing Truth, revealing the reality of good. A spiritual healer needs to always be aware of power. Is the divine power being accepted or refused? The choice is within you.

Refuse to be programmed by superstition. And whatever is your present happiness level, expect it to double. Whatever your present abundance, love, and blessings are, expect this to grow at exponential rates. Most of us do not experience life at greater levels than we expect due to our limited expectations.

Open the door to sustaining the thought that you deserve all good and that you deserve it all the time.

Open the door also to the fact that there is much more good coming to you, without any negative payment or backlash. Why is this?

Because in reality we are not becoming more of anything. Is Love becoming more loving through time, thought, desire, or event? No. Love is simply manifesting itself at the highest level of perfection at all times throughout eternity. Is this not your birthright as Love's Highest Self expression?

By refusing to accommodate or incorporate superstition, we can remove limitations and be open to far more possibilities of Love. Always remember to identify your Highest Self and rise above superstition. There is nothing standing between you and your infinite potential of love.

Common categories of *physical* false beliefs

In my healing practice, there are certain physical conditions that are common. I list them here so you can see that I also categorize these as false beliefs or illusions:

- fever
- infection
- inflammation
- disease
- blockage
- stoppage
- contagion
- deformity
- growth
- tear
- break
- cut
- injury
- congestion
- dysfunction
- pressure
- pain
- ache
- swelling
- fatigue
- imbalance
- deficiency
- age
- weakness
- defense-lessness
- stress
- history
- heredity

Every single belief you just read is untrue about you. It has never been true, is not true, and never will be true. These are all common beliefs I hear every week from people who call me. They are common to us at different times because they are part of the human, not divine, consciousness. And the human consciousness out-pictures what it believes.

Begin now to make your separation from false beliefs every time you become conscious of their association with you.

In fact, reviewing the list, did you find some of these thoughts to be presently familiar and ongoing in your own consciousness? Reject them now and stay alert to keep them dismissed as you begin to replace them with the opposite quality, which is your true, divine birthright.

Unless you define yourself each day and grow in your spiritual identity, you will find yourself *automatically* defined by beliefs.

False beliefs:

- Redefine you.
- Lead you away from your life purpose.
- Invade your health and well being.
- Interrupt your life fulfillment.
- Diminish your value and self worth.
- Impose on your spirituality.
- Vastly limit you.

False beliefs are recycled until we stop believing them and denounce them in exchange for Truth. In order to heal beliefs:

- Detach from the belief.
- Observe the belief as separate from you.
- Deny the belief.
- Affirm Love's Truth, overriding the belief.
- See yourself prevailing over the belief.
- Accept your beautiful identity as divine and therefore perfect, whole, and complete.

An example of healing a false belief of heredity

Many of my relatives have been plagued with bleeding hemorrhoids. Many of them had to have operations, even more than once in order to solve the problem.

When I started having this same problem, I began to pray, applying the principles of Love to the situation.

I reasoned that my heritage, as wonderful as it is, coming from two loving parents, did not begin there. My heritage is eternal.

I began to claim all that my eternal heritage means. I made lists to acknowledge my eternal heritage from Love, and gave deep gratitude that I knew this to be so.

There were many times over several years, when I prayed this way while having a bowel movement. I found that these prayers would, most often, control the situation, minimizing bleeding, inflammation, itching, and swelling. I noticed that, when I was emotionally going through something and stressed, it worsened and I had to pray more often. Eventually, there were days when I never even thought of it and the problem came less often.

Continuing in prayer, I recognized my true divine eternal heritage and named specifically to myself all that I have inherited. I was also very gentle with myself, and Love brought healing. No surgery was necessary and I felt cared for by Love throughout the healing process.

Another instance of false belief of heritage was healed when I began to discover a bone spur in my foot. Recalling that many of my relatives had surgery on this very problem – and I had been warned that this was a chronic problem in our family – I used the same method to heal it.

My prayers insisted on my perfection, reminding myself that I stand on my heritage with Love, and all my heritage is good, I found the pain and appearance of the problem left. Sometimes, I reminded myself of my heritage, as completely, not just partially, good. I reasoned that all my heritage is blessed and none of it is cursed. I knew this had to be true for all my relatives as well. As this thought became more prominent in my mind, it replaced the false belief. I was permanently healed. Through prayer, everything works in behalf of our healing.

These two instances – the hemorrhoids and bone spur – are wonderful proofs that our true and only heritage is divine. Both these were healed through spiritual means alone. Your heritage is completely good, never bad.

With DNA findings, we are more tempted than ever to believe that we are pre-doomed with coding that is both negative and positive from our ancestors. Yet the eternal, unchanging law of divine immunization is still supreme over all beliefs.

Today, when we are so capable of mass destruction through biological and nuclear means, it is deeply comforting to know where to turn for help for our real protection and defense.

Moving from false beliefs to spiritual wisdom leads to a life of healing and freedom in Love. In the next chapter we will address the number one most common false belief, fear.

Chapter 8

Healing Fear
with Love's Comfort

The belief we most suffer from every single day is fear. Fear is the root of all our problems. It clouds perceptions and interprets all the events of our lives unless we intervene with Love's healing Truth.

Each day in my healing practice, I feel like Mother Love. My heart opens wide and I comfort, nurture, calm, soothe, encourage, praise, and assure. I do this sincerely and continually. It is Love moving me to express caring compassion. I want to make things better. I want to bless. I want to end suffering.

Above all, a healer is a nurturer. Nurturing heals. Nurturing is what Love does.

There is not a person or animal or plant on earth that does not need or want nurturing. Why? Because nurturing and comfort take us to a healing place where there is no more fear.

We are so accustomed to living with fear that we rarely pay attention to fear until we experience an extra load of it. Then we become nervous, anxious, burdened, stressed, tired, overwhelmed, and sometimes depressed. Nearly everyone is running a deficiency of Love's nurturing.

When someone calls me and describes a problem, the first thing I do is offer comfort. This is not pity. It is compassion for their hardship, knowing that the problem will vastly improve once we turn to Love. I am literally moved by Love to help them. I care. My care wants to offer immediate comfort. That's how Love healing begins.

We are programmed to think that we will only feel comfort when a solution comes. Yet, in spiritual healing, it is preventive medicine to offer yourself comfort and nurturing as a first response to a problem and before the solution appears.

Comfort is not taken down from the shelf only on special occasions. Take comfort off the shelf permanently and use it continually every day, not only for yourself but for everyone. Everyone needs comfort. Learn how to give comfort. And teach your children how to comfort and be comforted.

Here is the wonderful truth behind what you are doing as a comforter. Every time you express comfort, you are uniting with Love and practicing your Highest Self. How valuable and powerful is that!

Let's now unpack the wonderful skills of a Love healer so you can become aware of what you most need to practice every day in healing yourself and others, ending fear.

A Love healer's skills that cancel fear

Assurance

When you are assured, you are confident, safe, secure, protected, and convinced. Express this by relying wholeheartedly on Love.

Calmness

When you are calmed, you are experiencing the energies of rest, quiet, peace, and stillness. Your calm presence will be healing for yourself and others.

Comfort

When you are comforted, you are consoled, free from worry, soothed, and joyful. Practice comforting yourself and others every day.

Encouragement

When you are encouraged, you feel uplifted, hopeful, buoyant, and bright, ready to go forward. When you express en-*courage*-ment, you are empowering and uplifting yourself and this offers healing love to others.

Nurture

When you are nurtured, you are fed with a steady diet of Love and you feel whole, complete, and abundantly loved. You will then know the value of offering nurturing love to others.

Praise

When you are praised, you feel worthy, loved, included, important, essential, and valued. Replace criticism, timidity, and judgments with praise. Praise heals.

Affirmations & denials

Often as a daily meditation – especially on days when I feel discouraged, nervous, or anxious – I use affirmations to comfort and calm myself. You can do this, too. For example:

- *I am* (nurtured, comforted, etc...)
- *I include* (assurance, encouragement, etc...)
- I have thoughts filled with (calm, praise, etc...)

Consider what is being displaced as a result of bringing in new knowledge based on Love. Let's use the following examples with the prefix "I am..." and apply these to you:

- I am assured, therefore, I am not insecure, alone, vulnerable, or unaided.
- I am comforted, therefore I am not distressed, disturbed, or troubled.
- I am calmed, therefore I am not nervous, agitated, stressed, hurried, or guilty.

- I am encouraged, therefore I am not discouraged, down, or depressed.
- I am nurtured, therefore I am not ignored, neglected, or unloved.
- I am praised, therefore I am not unworthy, guilty, blamed, unimportant, or condemned.
- I am peaceful, therefore I am not stressed, conflictive, oppressed, in pain, or disordered.

In addressing fear, I am continually re-phrasing my inner talk to align with Love's wisdom or reality. Here are some examples of how I use denials for healing fear. You can do this, too.

"Because I am Love's full expression, I am not..."

- Afraid – This is not me.
- Distressed – These are not my thoughts.
- Nervous – This is not my true condition.
- Worried – I cannot be made to believe that this problem or these thoughts are mine or belong to me.
- Burdened – This is not my true identity and I have divine authority to throw it out.

It is imperative to address and overcome fear on a daily basis. We address fear by dwelling on its opposite – Love – and not on fear itself. Here is how healing fear can make a difference.

Turning to Love in a crises

One evening, Scott and I were on the freeway headed home.

There were six lanes and we were in the far left speed lane, moving at about 75 mph. All of a sudden, I saw sparks flying from the rear of the car. In seconds it became a fire wall of sparks. We had to stop. Yet there was no where to pull off. Right there on this incredibly busy freeway, we stopped.

I'll make the story condensed. We had to negotiate a life threatening situation and every second meant life or death. Cars were headed straight for our car at 75 miles per hour.

Because it was night, they couldn't see us until seconds before reaching us. I was flagging every car, hoping that they would not only see me in time, but also hoping that the adjacent lane of heavy traffic would open up in the split second they had to move before crashing into us. It was one of the scariest times of my life.

The first thing Scott and I did when we got out of the car was pray, in order to calm our terror and hear the angels. Fear and tension were sky high. We were in great danger and so was every car on the freeway. I yelled affirmations, as we listened to Love's guidance, with traffic whirling past us.

In our quick investigation, we discovered that we had run over a large piece of steel grid that was stuck on the rear tire. It took a couple of tries to get it loose. In moments, we piled in the car and sped off. We felt Love's presence with us as we relied on it wholeheartedly.

Scott and I both feel that, because of the extreme danger and short time frame of finding the solution, we were divinely protected that night. And not only were we saved, but also every one around us. This is the power of turning to Love instantly in time of fear.

Sometimes I hear someone say they didn't have time to pray. You can't afford *not* to pray.

That was an example of an acute fear. What about chronic fear, which is far more common?

Fear in business

In addition to our work together as authors and teachers of Love, my husband also works as a real estate agent. And once a week, Scott, Bob (his real estate partner and friend), and I meet for lunch to discuss their business from both a practical and a metaphysical point of view.

There have been times when we met that business was almost dead and there was no end in sight. This brings up a lot of fear.

Turning to Love for guidance, we find over and over that we are calmed, renewed, and guided to do something specific that leads to success. Usually, it is in the form of an idea. And the idea will unfold even while fear continues to cause us to feel pressured.

Over the years, these ideas have contributed much to the lives of our clients and to the overall state of our financial well being.

We have been having these meetings for several years now. I asked Scott and Bob to rate their fear level at the time we started the meetings. And then I asked them to rate their current level of fear today.

The result was that their overall fear dramatically decreased over the period of time we'd been meeting. And we agreed that it was not because the money came in, though that was the eventual outcome on numerous occasions. The fear rating was lower because, even when times were hard, we felt Love sustaining us. At these lunches, we also experienced Love's deep comfort.

Addressing our fears in prayer supports our practical activity and leads to an overall plan for success. By failing to address our fears, we become paralyzed.

Daily, for over twenty five years, I have addressed all fears of financial scarcity by remembering Love's abundance to be my abundance. It doesn't need to be a labored "knowing."

When I began praying about it, my fear was great. Today my fear is generally very low. Can you see how, on a daily basis, addressing and overcoming fear with Love's healing comfort increases happiness and freedom from stress, burden, and worry?

A healer dissolves fears through massive comforting

In my healing practice, I continually turn clients toward Love for comfort and answers. The bulk of my practice calls have a great deal of fear and stress, whether or not there is a crises.

I have a regular number of people calling for healing illnesses, job crises, losses, travel safety, moving, conflict or discord in a relationship, grief, and nearly every type of problem. In each of these calls, I am first a Mother Nurturer. Everyone deserves comfort, especially when they consider their problem serious enough to call for professional help. I give comfort generously and this contributes largely to each healing.

We need to become experts at giving generous comfort and praise to lower everyone's level of fear as well as ours. This brings great healing to the earth and humanity. Babies, children, and young people need comfort and praise continually to know they are doing well and that their efforts count. So do adults. Learn to speak as Love by your words of comfort, encouragement, and praise to others.

Some people who call me are in a place of enormous life-shift. The changes they face are overwhelming with fear of the unknown.

The range of these types of problems is large, but they often involve a physical problem as well. For instance, due to a job lay off and the long-term effect of stress and worry, an old knee injury may return, or a new physical problem occur.

Or due to years of emotional abuse, the abused spouse may develop a chronic illness or dysfunction, or become physically incapacitated, even crippled. Unfortunately, I have seen this occur numerous times. I consider apathy, disrespect, and rudeness part of emotional abuse.

Litigation or divorce are accompanied by fear, and sometimes, by physical problems. Deep healing comfort and assurance are needed in order to face the unknown circumstances and to move through them with grace and wisdom while rebuilding lives. Problems can be a terrific struggle, but rewarding and healing when led by Love.

Whenever I receive a call about a chronic physical problem, I immediately begin to probe into the person's relationships. This is the biggest and most hidden area that alludes us, creating enormous fear.

Sometimes it is our relationship with ourselves that is the problem, practicing low self esteem, guilt, or self hatred. We can all do a better job of loving ourselves. And we need the support of those around us in order to do this.

Left turns in eternity

Healing often calls for massive shifts in our lives. I call these "eternity turns." What I mean by this is that a person has built his or her life on a structure for many years, a structure that begins to collapse. It is time for a "left hand turn in eternity." Time for a big change, many changes, even a complete transformation. This is a good thing. It may mean a change of job, relationship, or a move.

What has occurred is that we may have grown spiritually and changed dramatically over the years and the old forms of our lives no longer support our new, improved, and more evolved identity. I can spot this, though with great protest from the clients because they generally do not see the big picture of their lives outside their own immediate circumstances.

Or, in some cases, we may have grown spiritually, but our growth is stilted and remains within, not quite flowing into needed outward expression. Years of inward spiritual development, without outward change, eventually catches up with us. It can feel cataclysmic. Full transformation is then imperative for healing. This is what I call the need for making a sharp left hand turn in eternity.

We don't need to pass on in order to make large changes. Sometimes it takes more courage to live than to die. Since we don't escape learning all the lessons, we may as well learn our lessons right here. Can you grow and learn spiritually? Of course you can! And Love is here to guide you.

Each of us can develop the vision of Love that sees past the surface and understands the eternal solution.

Willingness to change brings healing

Basically, we are creatures of habit. We are not fond of change. Yet spiritual healing is synonymous with change. Change is unavoidable in spiritual healing. Perhaps the one way we could most help ourselves is to become willing and adaptive to change. We can become aware of ways that we resist change and begin to overcome them by opening up to consider change. In such cases, a willing and even joyful attitude is very helpful.

Please be alert to throw out self-condemnation and guilt. Change is not about failure for what we have not done. Think of change as a good thing and as a tool to offer you healing.

Children are perfect examples of how to change. They are generally flexible and quickly adaptable. They have a natural trust and willingness that causes them to be receptive to something new. As a result, they often heal quickly.

When you think about it, we are created by infinite, continuously unfolding Love. Change, and not stagnation, is our true nature. When we are willing, flexible, ready, and even eager to make changes where Love leads us, then we are most near our true, divine Self or Highest Self.

On the other hand, stubbornness and resistance to being in the next place of our evolutionary unfoldment works against our divine nature and our greatest good.

Would divine Love try to stop its eternal creative unfolding? Never. Love is infinite and, because of this, Love is continually fresh, new, non-repetitive, and birthing Itself with constant variety and expressiveness. This is also our true nature as divine expressions of Love.

We need not fear change. There is a divine and loving law sustaining every action. This law offers stability, constancy, and safety according to an infinite plan that aims to bless you.

We are most in harmony with Love when we are trusting the divine law to sustain us as we continue to change in accordance with Love's purpose for us.

The question is, what do we most trust? Resistance to change? Or acceptance and willingness to progress forth with Love? Change for the sake of change is meaningless. Change, led by divine direction, is healing.

Basically, when people call me for help, I am helping them to come into direct alignment with their Highest Selves. This is what offers healing, whether the problem is mild, acute, chronic, or terrifying. As a spiritual healer, I am the visionary on the case, and I count on Love every single minute to show me the way. It works.

As a mid-wife to the Soul, I am like a chiropractor who spots someone's need for re-alignment when the person doesn't have a clue. They think I am not hearing them when they describe a digestive problem, a chronic cough, pain in their body, or terror about money. I do hear them. But I hear more than that. I hear Love telling me what is behind the problem causing it.

There is nothing more beautiful to me than to see someone in humble readiness to learn the lessons of spiritual wisdom, and especially when the person is in great stress or pain. I already know the answer will be something they will ultimately love. I feel extremely blessed to be in this line of work.

Not every case, of course, calls for Soul realignment. But even on simple calls for help, there is a great need to be willing to shift to a higher place and turn to Love wholeheartedly for the answer. The sooner this is done, the sooner the fear begins to leave and healing takes place.

Holy work is the sweetest work in the world. God is our only Boss. I check in regularly to be sure that I am doing my job correctly. Healing work is joyful, blissful, inspirational, and happy. My clients and I often laugh our way through some of the problems, even during crises. It helps.

Learn to be a comforter and a nurturer

I hope that you will see the importance of nurturing in spiritual healing so that you will acknowledge that this is what you need in constant, large amounts. And that you, too, can nurture and comfort others generously, as generously as you yourself would want.

I am sure that, as you are reading this book, there are at least three things in your life that concern you greatly.

At this very moment, I encourage you to place the book down, pause, and offer yourself generous comfort, encouragement, praise, calm, and even forgiveness. Let Love pour out to you right where the concerns are. Do it now. Make it a daily habit.

Then call or talk to someone you love – or someone who needs love – and pour out comfort as if you were Love Itself. You are! Observe the healing effect that follows.

Just because you don't see the result of nurturing and comfort, please do not assume your Love efforts are wasted or given in vain. I guarantee you they are not.

If you began today offering comfort and nurture to every single person you saw for the rest of your life, you would be offering monumental healing towards a better world. The world is starving for comfort, longing to be relieved of fear. Help them as a Love healer.

Love is the healer of fear.

Chapter 9

Love's Reality

As we heal, it is necessary that we are willing to shift our thoughts, perceptions, and attitudes to a higher place. In fact, it is more than that.

Let me take you straight to the place of radical healing. This is where you need to go – and stay for sustained periods – for healing. And it is the happiest, most powerful, blissful, growing place you will ever be.

Here it is. Healing begins with sustaining the vision of your divinity.

That's it. It's that simple. The rest is figuring out the details of what that means. You can trust Love to show you in depth. Love is your guide. Identifying yourself with a divine origin and nature is exactly how healing takes place. Rather than Love coming to our reality to improve it, in healing, we are going to Love's reality. Love is the place that always heals.

In this chapter I will help you to see this more clearly.

First of all, healing begins the moment you think of yourself as divine. Healing occurs as you see and explore your divinity, while allowing this understanding to expand even more in your consciousness. This new understanding is life transforming. As this identity exercise is sustained during periods of growth and insight, divine Truth will take deep root in your consciousness. Healing then occurs naturally.

Awareness of our divinity is the basis of every healing. Yet, at the core of every human problem, our divinity is in question: "Are you really divine? Who are you really? How are you really?" Has your divinity been re-defined by a problem? Are you to believe that, in addition to your divine Self, you are also an individual who has a problem? The healing answer is "No." This would be an imposition on your divine Selfhood.

As we begin to discover our real selfhood to be divine (contrary to being the self with a problem), then we are claiming and owning the healing, even before it appears outwardly.

As healing manifests, we are free in our divine Self, unopposed, having worked out the contradiction to our real identity. The key to healing is to place all your focus and energy on your divine Selfhood. Not just saying it, but coming to understand, apply and grow in it, and not allow yourself to be re-defined as an individual with a problem.

I am trying to put this in as simple terms as possible so you can grasp ultimate healing concepts. When put to the test, you will find these concepts to be more than just theory. They prove themselves. Healing works.

Allow Love to reveal your divinity to you

Are you a divine being, created by Love? Then the problem is edited out. Love's all presence precludes any problem.

Or, are you an individual with a problem who is struggling to be the divine Self? In successful spiritual healing, all roads lead back to your correct identity. I know of no exceptions.

In healing, you realize that you are a divine being whose presence is Love.

This may sound far fetched to you, but with my background of thousands of healings, I can tell you that this is the core place for all healings. Your sole task is to ask Love to guide you in revealing your divinity. Then focus attention on listening and knowing exactly what Love is saying and in what ways Love is guiding you in the healing. Practice seeing yourself as divine.

It is helpful to journal what Love is imparting to you. This helps you stay in focus and also helps to reveal that you really are in touch with the divine messages which you asked for and are now receiving. These messages are healing you. I have journaled years of daily notes from God.

Think of your divinity and hold this thought in sacred trust as you begin to let go of all else that stands in your way, such as identifying with a problem. Divine Love is not identifying itself with a problem. Learning to think so differently about yourself is the equivalent of a river changing course, moving in an entirely different direction. As Love healers, we stand ready to happily change course in order for our currents to flow with Love.

So the direction of your thought that rehearses the problem, all that surrounds it, and all that keeps you stirred about it, is the direction that is preventing you from contemplating your exemption from the problem.

Healing is similar to singing a beautiful song in a chorus and coming to the note that requires a sustained tone while the other singers are singing other notes in the background. Your only role is to sustain your note. Vibrate and sing your song of healing at your highest level, the level of Love's healing. Sing your note, even if other notes around you are off key.

As you sustain the thought of yourself as divine, your healing will require you to act out your new, permanent self. Your divinity realized more fully, and consistently acted on, is all that is needed for your healing.

Never assume that the healing is one step. It may be many. It may be far beyond your present comprehension. It doesn't matter. You are being led by Love. Prepare to sing and sing and sing, and enjoy every single note, trusting that you are doing the most right thing for your healing as you are little by little guided by Love all the way home to the healing.

Healing is an inside job.

A personal example of a profound Love healing

Let me share with you how I applied all this in my life.

About fifteen years ago, I had a car accident which resulted in an injured leg. The injury was severe. It was a frightening experience but I learned, as I applied these truths, that Love was with me all the way. Here is what occurred.

While at a car wash, I hurriedly got out of my car and neglected to set it in park. The car began to roll towards a line of cars in front of me.

I realized, as my car began to roll forward, that it was going to hit the car in front of me and set off a chain reaction of additional cars being hit. As I struggled to get back into my car, I stupidly tried, for a split second, to drag the car and slow it with my leg that was stuck outside the car. My leg was going the opposite direction of the car and so it took the entire momentum of the car.

At that moment, I knew I had made a dreadful mistake. Something shot through my leg and I had a strange sensation that I never felt before. The power of the car against my leg had damaged it, but I couldn't stop to assess my injury. I still had to stop my car.

Fear set in. Trauma set in. People started running towards me to see if I was okay. As I placed the car in park, I stopped. Assuring the people that I was fine, trying so hard to hold back tears, I got the car turned around, and headed home, only minutes away.

I didn't want others to call for an ambulance. I was so accustomed to success in spiritual healing that I just wanted to get home and pray.

I cried and trembled all the way home. My hip, thigh, knee, and foot were all in great pain. I knew I had internally torn parts of my leg and felt I had perhaps done damage to a couple bones in my foot. I was terrified at what I had done.

Once I was home, I was unable to walk and had to drag myself to the front door and down to my bedroom into bed. Looking at my leg, I saw that it was already terribly swollen.

I immediately called a fantastic professional spiritual healer to back me up in the healing. Fear persisted. So did pain.

The biggest question I faced was, "Should I go to the hospital? Or should I even try to heal it?" The next biggest question was just as immediate, "How can I endure the pain? And will I be able to heal it?"

Judging from what I intuited, I felt I would probably require several surgeries. Could Love heal this?

I reviewed my several years of spiritual healing victories – including chronic infections and a second growth in my breast. Generally, everything in my family and my healing practice had been successfully healed through the years. The record was great. However, I'd never come across such a terrific challenge as this.

Healing the pain was foremost in my mind. I had healing books, the Bible, spiritual hymns, and poems in bed with me. I could barely even think for myself but I found that, by making the effort to pray and listen for angels, I had moments of insight, comfort, and even inspiration as the hours went by. Yet the pain persisted. Still, I contemplated and read anything that could help me to stay focused on my spirituality.

It was a miracle, but that night I slept soundly all night. When I awoke the pain was still there. I cried a lot in fear and worry. I continued to pray and listen.

By early afternoon, almost twenty four hours after the accident, I picked up a hymnal and begin to read the inspiring verses. Verse after verse caused me to feel the power of God and my divine oneness with Love. I spent the entire afternoon with the hymnal. I was so interested in what I was learning as I listened to Love that I lost track of time. The intrusions of pain came less often. This was the result of all the prayer.

By the end of that afternoon, all pain had totally left my body. It never returned. I was so relieved for this part of the healing. Though my leg was still very swollen and felt and looked very strange, the first sign of healing was the total removal of pain. This helped calm me, but I still had a long way to go. And I couldn't walk.

Every day I asked myself, "Should I go to the hospital for treatment?" In being divinely led each day, I felt complete in the work, sensing that it was sufficiently progressing forth my healing.

I continued to pray, study, and listen, while food was brought to me by people who attended me during the day, sometimes by a friend and other times by a person I hired. I continued to focus on my divinity and to separate as best I could from all the thoughts and sensations of my predicament and memory of the accident.

Within a couple of weeks, the fear had come down from a 10 on a scale between 1 – 10, perhaps to a 9. I was still very concerned about my being able to heal this. Would I be able to walk again?

A couple more weeks went by. I slowly began to think with a little less attachment to the problem and more of Love's true reality. This is one way I measured my progress. I knew it was important to be objective about the experience and have as much non-attachment to the injury as possible.

Here is the result of my pouring in weeks of hours and hours of prayers, thoughtful study, and listening about my relationship with God regarding my identity as Love's Highest Self.

It began dawning on me, about the third week, that for weeks and months leading up to the accident, I had a growing sense of feeling stuck in my healing practice. It was actually worse than that. I secretly felt that I'd gone as far as I could as a healer. I was not happy.

Healing was all I ever wanted to do with my life, but the practice was proving to be very burdensome, listening to long conversations from people describing their problems who didn't care much about listening to what I had to say. I felt like I'd become a dumping ground and my joy for healing had left. Yet what was I to do with the rest of my life? My practice was crippled. My body was acting out my life predicament.

One day, lying on the bed, I felt a new sensation. It was uncomfortable, but it wasn't painful. The first time this happened I was very concerned. What did it mean? Alarmed that the pain may be returning, I turned to Love. As I prayed, the message from Love was surprising. I intuited that spiritual surgery was being performed. I was both amazed and relieved! Listening and intuiting is indispensable to understand healings. I intuited that tissue in my leg was pulling together to heal. It turned out to be true.

Because my need for healing was so great, I had to spiritually reach higher and stretch further than I'd ever gone before. During this period, I had a divine revelation. This revelation stayed with me throughout the healing and ever since, and over the years it has carved out a new picture of Love's reality for me.

The revelation, as revelations tend to be, was very simple, yet profound. I felt that Love was revealing Itself to me in a new way and a huge way that had never dawned on me with so much meaning.

Love showed me that the *only* presence is the presence of Love. Imagine! Right now, the only presence is the presence of Love! Can you fathom such an illuminating thought as this? This means that the place you now occupy which you call your own presence is actually occupied by Love. And you are *that* presence.

This means that the place that appears to be occupied by trouble and danger is actually, in truth, Love's presence. This leads us to look far deeper into what we presently call our reality. This calls on each of us to be Love visionaries.

In spiritual healing, the demand is great to see past the obvious, superficial appearance of things that we call real.

Go past all appearances and require yourself to see divinity everywhere. This is your divine right. And this is necessary for healing.

I adored thinking of this revelation, applying it to the predicament of my leg which appeared to be so real. Love wanted me to know that its presence is all there is. And Love's presence is total reality, even though it appeared that I was on the bed suffering from an injury, and trying hard to have a healing, with much worry and concern about the outcome.

The revelation was very comforting and healing to me. I could see that, if Love was all present, then Love was all that existed. After all, how could another presence exist if there is only one Presence?

If this is true, I concluded, then everything everywhere is Love, and we are all Love. Love is the only identity! The only Self! The only existence! The only condition! We are all the One Presence of Love. This was like medicine to my Soul! I thought of it continually and allowed it to expand. I felt that even the mere contemplation of this was healing me. And it was.

This new view of reality was brought forth from Love. It was not intellectual as much as a result of my prayers. It changed many of my thoughts and attitudes, including my professional spiritual practice. I no longer had a view of my clients working against me, draining me. I now had a new view that we were all one and therefore mutually beneficial to each other. These applications came effortlessly.

While I was healing in bed for this entire period, I continued to take calls from clients asking for my healing help. I found that I could speak up and interrupt people's long stories and become a prominent influence for healing. This was a first for me. And this presented the very opening I needed, a light of hope. I slowly began to take charge of my practice. I began to see the light at the end of the long tunnel.

As the new concept took root, after all these weeks, I realized that I was being healed.

In all, I was in bed for about eight weeks. When I emerged, I was a new person with a huge opening to go forward in my life as a happy healer.

Within a few months, I was back running on the tennis court with total ease. The leg has never given me a problem. And, since that time, I have been a healer in charge of her healing practice.

The infrastructure of a healing

Today, in my healing practice, I ask Love to show me the healing's individual infrastructure. For example, the infrastructure – or the healing behind the physical healing – is often the real thing I am healing. In my situation, what I most suffered from was not a leg injury, but the belief that I was suffering from harm in my life. The result was that I was stuck and unable to go forward until I changed my ways.

Where are you most stuck in your spiritual evolution? Does your Soul believe it is stuck?

I often do healing strategy with clients. From eternity, we view the big picture of the healing. It's like having a map of the healing. It is intuited by asking Love for specific guidance, "What are we really healing here?"

Please note. This is often where people feel most discouraged and, instead of listening further to Love, they get buried in guilt. This is where I send you my greatest support and encouragement for you to press on. Please know that, in these dark moments, you are not alone. Every compassionate heart on earth is with you, caring and supporting. Love surrounds you. I often, in the middle of the day, pause and love all on the planet who are struggling. I pour out my heart to them with empowering love. You can do this too.

Regarding the healing of my leg injury, you may ask, "But couldn't all this learning have taken place under medical care?"

I don't share this healing so you will see a way of avoiding a visit to the doctor, nor for you to feel that you failed if you do. In fact, I deeply support anyone's decision to use medical care, and some of the clients who call for my help are under medical care. Yet, with or without medical care, we have to eventually learn the deeper lessons that heal life's obstacles.

I share this healing story to show you the scope of spiritual healing from the inside out. And to expose you to the power of attuning to Love's reality, and to see the power of seeing yourself as a divine expression of Love. I have found spiritual healing to be reliable and safe, even during crises. I never, however, take this for granted.

Looking on this healing experience, let me ask you a question. What was real? The accident and injury? Or my divinity? I had to insist on the divine reality until the false beliefs yielded to Love.

I learned that, as I focused solely on Love to show me the healing, I was led to see that only Love is real. The thought and experience of the accident and injury slowly receded as I gained new views of myself *as* Love. This is the true record of me in eternity. This view progressed forth my healing each day and led to the final healing.

Who am I? Who are you? We exist as Love.

When we come into the powerful healing light of Truth, we realize that it is radically different than the way we are accustomed to viewing reality.

We want Love's reality to permeate every aspect of our lives and allow this to awaken and transform us. This is entirely up to us. This is our call to find where we resist Love and Love's presence. It is our responsibility to call forth Love into our hearts and our minds and to bring this forth daily into our lives.

Visualize and trust the following as true.

At the precise core of your greatest challenge at this moment, Love is there operating as a law of healing. Love is enlightening this place with comfort, assurance, strength, renewal, and transformation.

In what appears as the darkest place of your life, Love is operating as the brightest Light, transforming the entire place into a place of healing Light.

Love has yet to have met its first real challenge. There has never been any problem too hard for Love to heal. And there never will be. Awaken to the presence of Love at this very moment and experience its healing light.

Healing is the revealing of divine reality

There is only one reality. It is divine Love's Allness. It's as though real life is hidden behind a veil. When we lift the veil of our ingrained but false perceptions, we see Love's beautiful reality. It was there all along! We don't have to change what is in front of the veil, or even re-create it. Just lift the veil. That's where Love's reality is and that's where all your healings are. Waiting for you! Waiting within!

This is exactly how I was healed from the accident.

It is important to remember:

- In healing, we are not creating something new.
- We are not trying to get rid of a problem.
- We are not trying to change reality. We are recalling reality.
- We are not responsible for creating a new reality.
- We do not have a burden of having to produce a healing.
- The healing is never "outside of you." It is always within you unfolding. Always. Lift the veil and you will see.
- Healing is revealed to you as you become willing to see more of the divine reality revealed, in place of the problem.
- Healing is the understanding that you are the expression of God. And, therefore, perfection is normal and natural to you at all times. Perfection is your divine right.
- Healing is the experience of knowing that divine Love is not mysterious, but know-able, real, present, and available.

Your innate perfection

When we become quiet and listen for divine Truth, our natural state of divinity and wellness is revealed. Then we discover that what we consider to be a problem is not part of our self. Problems disappear in proportion to the inner dawning of our true spiritual and perfect self. It doesn't seem logical, but it's the way of spiritual healing.

The divine change that occurs in healing prayer is in our own mind and heart. Your consciousness – open to Love – is the beginning of all healing.

When we spend time each day with Love, we experience Love as already present. Your experience with this Presence causes healing.

When people are healed through spiritual means, it looks as though they sufficiently used their spirituality in order to transform their condition to a better state. This is accurate only at a superficial level.

At a deeper metaphysical level, they used their spirituality to awaken from a darkened state to an enlightened state. Problems are left behind as we emerge into Love's reality.

In an enlightened state, problems do not exist.

Underlying all appearances of a problem is Love's law of reality fully operating as a law of perfection to you every moment. To be in touch with this scientific law of perfect being, we need to remove the mental limitations that mask reality from us.

Your objective in spiritual healing is to allow your spirituality, or Love's divine Self, to prevail over the belief of a problem, thereby dissolving the problem. The highest objective of a spiritual healer is to uncover the great facts of existence and live life from this Highest Point of awakened being.

Why does spiritual healing work? Because it is true that the only and all existence is Love.

Love is all that exists

Love's All presence means that Love is:
- The only real condition or circumstance
- The only consciousness or intelligence
- The only law
- The only truth

- The only identity or Self
- The only reality
- The only creator or cause

For healing guidance, always ask Love what to think, without assuming you know the answer in advance.

For a healing reality-check, ask yourself, "Is this Love's reality?" Let your evaluation of what is true come from divine Love. Ask yourself, "Is this how Love sees my situation?" If the answer is "No," ask:

- Love, how do You see this?
- Love, what are You causing me to think about this?
- Love, how are You acting through me right now?

You may find it hard or impossible to accept that Love is the only reality. Yet the history of our civilization is our constantly changing perception of reality, rather than reality changing.

Eternity is now

We feel pressured. We are tired of struggle, suffering, anxiety, and burden. "When will I be healed?" We want to know!

Yet healing has nothing to do with time. Love and time have nothing to do with each other. Eternity is measured by Love's unfoldments. There is no time in eternity.

We can drop the pressure of time in order to experience greater peace during healing.

Think of yourself in this eternal moment. You existed before this earth experience. You will continue to exist after this earth experience. You have always existed in Love. You and Love are forever. In Love's reality, there is no beginning and no end. Forever is a healing place. Forever is healthy and real.

Every moment in your life is a moment in Love's eternity. Now is forever.

Affirm to yourself this healing statement: "The all-presence of Love is my life and I am eternal."

Healing is a time for loving and not judging ourselves

We heal best when we are loving ourselves and gently easing ourselves through to the new place which Love is providing. Since healing often means change, we can focus on how Love is showing us to go higher and we can accept that it is okay to be on a learning curve for growth.

In healing, we look inward, listen to angel thoughts, and evaluate things in our life with a fresh perspective. We intuit where the problem lies and what we are being led to do about it. It is a time of great inspiration.

This, then, means that healing is not a time when we take the attitude, "What did I do wrong?" We don't judge or condemn ourselves, or accept guilt because we have a problem. The experience of a challenge does not make you unworthy. In fact, this is a time you can love yourself twice as much.

Healing is not a time when we pray only once and wait the rest of the day for a healing – waiting without any thought towards the healing changes needed. All of these would be counter to healing and not Love's reality.

In healing problems that have been with us for a while, we can take the attitude that we are having an opportunity to take a giant step forward in eternity. "Eternity steps" are earned through prayer, awareness, willingness to listen and grow, trust, and go higher. These are the building blocks of your deepening spirituality and they aid you most as a monumental healer. Remember, Love is with you.

You can love the fact that spiritual healing is freeing you beyond any place you have been to date, enabling you to enjoy life with greater wisdom and power. This will make you a valuable Love healer to others with the lessons of wisdom you have learned.

Yes, but...

When your problem does not readily improve, it is often fear, ignorance, or someone's adverse treatment of you which are holding back the healing. This does not mean you are guilty or wrong. This means it is time to grow. How? Love, listen, pray, practice awareness, learn, and change. Ask Love how to do this.

I often have people calling with a list of problems. In response, I will talk about Truth. Then I may hear, "Yes, but..."

They do not see the correlation between their problem and Truth. "You must not understand. What does Truth have to do with it? This is a *real* problem." Really? Think again.

Let me take you to the solid place in thought where healing always occurs. As a spiritual healer, I have to be ready for calls with any degree of seriousness, including catastrophe and crises. They come often.

In order to offer the most powerful and immediate experience of healing when calls come in, I practice thinking of myself as the mind of God, looking out on all infinity. This is where I go, over and over. I identify all that I am envisioning as spiritual.

I see myself and all others as perfect and seeing ourselves as perfect, and seeing each other as perfect. I practice knowing that I, and we, are composed of infinite ideas, unfolding. I practice seeing the infinity of these ideas simultaneously interrelating with purpose. I see Love in all this unfoldment, filling every nook of reality. I call this pinnacle healing!

Below is a meditation to help you practice the perfect place of healing – your true identity, Love's reality. Let these be your very own thoughts as you read the following powerful meditation. Be in the consciousness of a Love healer. Let "I, Love" be also *you*:

I, Love...

"I, Love, look out upon my infinite Self. All I see is Love, everywhere. I am Love. My Love creates all that exists and all that has ever existed or ever will exist. I am the only I, us, we, and self. I, Love, am All.

I, Love, am eternally unfolding with creativity. I evoke the unfolding of My law of love. My thoughts are love. My actions are only love. I effortlessly unfold my design and plan of beauty and perfection within each moment.

Forever rested, I, Love, include all peace. All aspects of My Perfect Beloved Peaceful Self are marvelous, wonderful, magnificent, grand, and glorious. As Love, this is what I look like.

I, Love, am forever filled with joy. I bubble and exude the full realm of joy. I smile. My joy is incapable of lessening. My joy is a perpetual blessing to Myself, to My entire Allness.

I, Love, create and comprehend all wisdom. I am the only mind or consciousness. From my all-knowingness springs forth all intelligence, inspiration, illumination, and understanding. I, Love, am incapable of not knowing.

I, Love, am filled with My substance of love. All love is Me. When I see Myself, I see love. When I feel Myself, I feel love. Love's perfection, completeness, and wholeness are My essence and nature. This is who I am.

I, Love, am the Source of all being. All being is My Love Being. I am all present. Within My all presence is all life and all power. I am the only Cause of all that exists. I alone create the all and only Effect.

I, Love, am complete goodness. My entire endless Self manifests complete innocence, fairness, and beloved presence. I, Love, am incapable of being less than all good. I am forever welcome.

My infinite Love Being is without borders and never ends. I, Love, am self-renewing and continually birthing fresh, brilliant ideas, which I send forth with purpose and fulfillment. Each individual Love idea is united with all My ideas. I am all living and all life. I am abundant. No part of me can be limited or confined.

I am infinite Mother Love. As Mother, I give My infinite comfort, appreciation, nurturing, and calmness to every aspect of My Being, all at once. I am filled with worth and value. I, Love, am all family, united. I am One.

I, Love, am the radiant Light of Love. My brilliance is inspiring, beautiful, intelligent, enlightening, and forever. This and every moment, I shine with eternal brightness. I am incapable of darkness.

I, Love, am the all and only I AM. There exists nothing in addition to Me."

Chapter 10

Love's Powerful Healing Energies

I remember, after I had been in the healing practice for a few years, that my clients sometimes would comment on how powerful I was. Me? I heard myself described as strong and powerful. I had no idea that this is how I was being perceived. I wasn't sure that I liked it either. I even thought, "Was this necessary?"

Asking Love what I should think about it, I learned something about Love that I had not taken into consideration. Love's healing energies are, indeed, powerful.

As we come closer to Love, we take on more of Love's healing qualities, including its power. This discovery has been helpful.

Love's inspiration generates an enormous flow of healing power. A healer needs a constant Niagara Falls flow of inspiration and its powerful energies.

Yin energies

So far in this book, you have experienced the power of Love's soft, gentle, nurturing, flowing, healing energies. I have equated them to Mother

Love's nurturing power. You could also call this the yin energies of Love.

In Chinese philosophy, yin is the feminine force or principle of the universe. It is contrasted to the yang, which we will also discuss. I think of Mother Love whenever I think of yin energies. Mother Love assures, calms, comforts, encourages, nurturers, and praises. In healing children, I nearly always stay in yin energies. Children need a great deal of calm assurance and they generally respond swiftly to Love's nurturing qualities.

Here is an example of healing with yin energies. I recall a woman leaving a voice message for me and explaining that, for several months, she had not been able to hear in one of her ears. She requested that I pray for her over the next few days concerning this problem. I did.

After a few days, she again left another message asking for a couple more days of prayer. As of yet, I had not personally spoken with her. Again, I continued praying.

The following day, she called and we had a lengthy talk about her marriage and about a new disturbance in her life of her husband's deception, lying to her about their money and defaulting on payments.

In response to her anger and disappointment in him, as well as her new fear regarding the control of their money, I utilized powerful yin energies in a very natural way. I comforted her with the assurance that Love has a plan for healing her ear as well as for healing the problem with her husband.

As I shifted her thought to see him in a higher light, I felt divinely directed in every word that was softly pouring forth from me, describing him as Love sees him. However, it was difficult for me to speak because she wasn't listening. Instead, she was contradicting much of what I was saying.

I lovingly explained that her hearing needed to be active with divine listening. Her divine ear needed to be open and receptive. It also meant she needed to stop talking adamantly about the problem, insisting it was all true. Her attitude shifted during the conversation. She began listening. The words I was led to speak were being received. I felt healing was occurring.

Two days later, she called and reported that her ear was fully capable of hearing and she was using what had been her deaf ear on the phone and could hear me perfectly.

She also said that her husband, who she described as impossible to live with and stubborn, had apologized to her for his behavior and said that he was going to change. She told me that, in all their years of marriage, he'd only apologized a couple of times. She felt relieved and joyful.

Yang energies

In my healing work, I also call on a different energy that is equally Love's healing power.

In the Chinese philosophy, yang is the masculine force or principle in the universe, and you will increasingly feel this powerful energy as you read on.

There are times when you will need to rally and utilize stronger healing energies, with greater determination, and with a healing attitude of strongly claiming the presence of healing. You may even feel defiant, boldly resisting opposition to beliefs that are holding back the healing.

It is important not to withhold the needed extra power necessary for any healing.

For example, I expressed yang healing energies to a woman with whom I occasionally played tennis. She was a new mother. Her baby had been taken to the hospital with enormous swelling throughout his body. His condition was serious.

Her call for help was hysterical. I'll never forget her desperation as I listened to her voice over the phone. It took a moment for me to understand who she was and what she was saying. Through tears she was yelling, "You've got to save my baby! Don't let my baby die!"

In response to her cries for help, I recall flooding her with forceful healing truth. Feeling a rush of tremendous inspiration, I was adamant that the child was not going to die. I vehemently voiced that Love was protecting her child and nothing could harm him. I spoke to her for a brief time in this passionate manner, trying to talk over her protests of his pain and death.

I felt defiant, as though the belief of death would have to cross my path in order to get to the child, and Love and I would not allow that to happen. My immediate, spiritual, powerful stand for the child's right to live came from the depth of my being. At once, the mother felt the power of these healing energies. So did I.

I must add that, when I heard the description of this child and the mother's desperation, I didn't become mechanical and think, "I need yang energies in order to heal this." It was an unconscious decision to allow divine power to come through me and through my voice. I was responding to my compassion for her and the child.

It was with full receptivity that I opened up totally to hear what the angels were telling us at that dire moment. I wanted to respond to what she felt was critical.

My voice was strong and unwavering. My attitude was set and clear. I meant every word that I was being led to speak. We both heard the confidence and it inspired us.

Oddly enough, I assured her that her baby could not be poisoned and that he was pure. I try never to judge what I am led to say. This was no exception.

Though I thought it strange to be discussing poison, I trusted it was right.

She was calmed by my forceful attitude and by my words. After we hung up, I continued to pray.

The next day, her husband called to tell me that the baby was fine. They discovered that their son was highly allergic to a medicine they were giving him for a cold. His body had been treating the medicine like a toxic poison and couldn't overthrow it. However, after the call to me, the entire body swelling subsided without any medical aid. The child was protected throughout the entire ordeal and no further medicine was given or needed.

I have noticed a pattern among some people who use my healing services for the first time. They are reluctant to admit the healing. I never heard back from the mother, which I thought was odd since she called for help and expected me to save her baby. Months later, I ran into her at the tennis court and, though she was warm and friendly, she never mentioned the incident and never thanked me.

I think that, because our culture is not accustomed to asking for, expecting, or paying for healing prayer, there is a tendency not to acknowledge it, even when someone has been greatly benefited by it. It is my deepest hope that this changes.

Blending yin and yang energies

Although the yin or yang energies may not be predictable as to which you will need, they are always there for you, in full, abundant amounts.

I observe myself most often using yang energies in three different areas:

- When the need is urgent.
- When the person is protesting against truth.

- When there is a need to have a break through and the softer energies are not enough.

Both these divine energies – yin and yang – are equally powerful and healing. The decision on which energies to utilize will be made for you as you are led in your healing work. Often it may be both. Be open to both as you are directed by Love's healing inspiration.

In my daily spiritual practice of people calling me for healing, I most often utilize and blend yin and yang energies. For example, some people who call for healing may call once and be healed. Others may call for sustained help.

During these healing Love calls, Love leads me both to comfort and also to pronounce truth. It's indescribably beautiful to feel Love's healing comfort and nurturing combined with Love's muscle of truth and rebellion against all disease, illness, and evil.

Biblical angels

It is interesting that two of the archangels mentioned in the Bible are similar to energy healers.

Gabriel, for example, is the angel that leads multitudinous angels in energies of ministering love. This angel is the equivalent to the yin energies.

Michael, on the other hand, is the angel that leads multitudinous angels in energies of powerful strength and defense.

I have never thought to myself that I will consciously call on one angel or the other. They are always with us and they offer exactly what we need at the time. I rely on them every single day for healing. I love them.

In the Bible, there is a lovely passage about angels that stays with me. It offers important information about angels, too.

"And suddenly there was with the angel a multitude of heavenly host praising God and saying, Glory to God in the highest, and on earth peace, good will to men."

This tells us that one angel is accompanied by a multitude of other angels, messaging Love. A Bible translation interprets the word heavenly as *celestial* and the word host as an *army of luminaries*.

Isn't it comforting to know that an army of celestial luminaries accompanies you right now and they are messaging Love's thoughts to you for your healing?

Power wattage versus power outage

As healers, we need to stay in Love's healing power, yet we often give away our power – power that could be claimed for ourselves and exempt us from feeling fear and suffering. Let's explore common areas where we give our power away. We'll start with the simpler ones and go to the more subtle ones.

Lost objects – We rehearse, "It's lost! I can't remember where I was when I last had it with me. I can't find it. Is it here? Or here?" We run through our house, pockets, car, purse, looking behind and under everything. Our actions are contradicting our much needed affirmations which could be:

"I include the idea of this object. This idea is immediately available to me. I am listening quietly and confidently to Love to be led."

We have a rule in our house. Nothing, ever, is lost. We never admit to loss. And we are always finding what appears to be lost by following the instruction above. Think about it. This means we cannot lose anything – our health, our mind, our supply, our love. We need never give our power away to losses of any kind.

Reacting to loud noises – When a dog has been repeatedly barking, or neighbors are noisy for a long period, or a baby keeps crying and crying, we are tempted to give away our power. We rehearse, "This noise is stressing me out! This dog, baby, or person is irritating me! I am about to explode!" These actions are contradicting our much needed affirmations such as:

"My peace is divine and cannot be invaded. What appears as a loud noise is calmed by Love's calming presence which reminds me that I am calm and peaceful by nature and so are they. Nothing can disturb us. Whatever are the needs of this baby or dog can be met by Love now. And my needs are equally met. We are united with Love's peace and the belief of irritating noise is outside us."

I can't tell you how many times I have used this divine direction for healing irritating noises. It is warming to know that, as I pray for the dog next door or the baby seated with its mother behind me in the airplane, my prayers are having a calming effect. They always do too.

Are these examples familiar?

Here are a few more.

Sleepless nights – We give away our power every time we make the affirmation, "I'm so tired! I didn't get a good night's sleep." A state of tiredness or fatigue tends to repeat itself all day in our mind.

We can refresh ourselves with some of the following affirmations to replace the repetitious thought of being tired, worn out, drained, or fatigued:

"Love is forever resting, and so am I. Love and I are totally rested. My consciousness is filled with rest. Each thought unfolds with rest, revealing my state of full restfulness. At all times, I include complete rest. My restful thoughts and actions are unbroken and without interruption."

Hidden evil – Nothing is more draining to your spiritual power and energy than hidden evil. Evil is a belief of duality, as though there are two realities rather than one. It takes full energy to continually defend yourself and stand guard against a person's insult, disrespect, accusation, anger, manipulation, or put down to you. It could be so subtle or so familiar to you that you don't realize it.

When evil is hidden from us or left unaddressed, we enable it to continue. It often occurs because our motive is to please others, keep things harmonious, win approval, or make someone happy. Other reasons we don't address evil are that we don't want to be unkind or get into an argument. Or we may even be afraid of confrontation. Or we may say, "I do protest but it doesn't do any good."

We may find ourselves feeling anxious or nervous and not know why. By ignoring evil, however, we may abandon ourselves and allow ourselves to be harmed, without knowing that the reason we are harmed is from unaddressed evil. This is a big area where we suffer from giving away our power.

Our naiveté lets in a great deal of misery. Many loving people have no idea what it costs them personally. I see this often in the healing practice.

It is helpful to silently affirm to yourself, "I am willing to address evil and not be fooled by it, nor try to avoid it. I know that by addressing evil, I am standing in the law of Love that says I am not here to enable others to neglect their responsibility of goodness. I am not here to suffer any penalty for other people's failure to do right. I am willing to take a stand for myself now. I recognize the need for my stand to be effective."

We will discuss the problem of evil more thoroughly in a later chapter.

Bad news – We've all experienced bad news. It comes in a phone call, a report, tests, a knock at the door, on TV, or correspondence. Regardless of how it comes, the question is, "Will you give your power away to it and agree that your power will not come back until after the problem has been solved?" Remember, you have a choice.

Will you tell yourself that you are now re-defined and your Highest Self no longer defines you? Because of the news, will you now be "a person who is afraid, sad, suffering, and telling others your bad news?" Or will you bring your healing light to the problem, while allowing yourself to awaken to a higher place with Love's divine healing guidance?

This doesn't mean, of course, that you skip your need to offer yourself generous comfort, hope, and encouragement. Of course you will offer that to yourself in large gulps. But as you do, you can also remember that the problem need not re-define you as someone with a problem or a need to constantly rehearse your new story to others. It is helpful, however, to share with a loving friend who can give you healing comfort and support.

Look ahead and accept Love's healing in advance even as you move into it.

Ask Love, "Love, what are you telling me? I rise to Your healing presence and listen to know your view of and solution to the entire problem."

In every case throughout your life, you can always bring the Light of your Highest Self and shine Love's healing light into the appearance of darkness until it disperses.

You can say, "My Highest Self is defined only by Love, which is my true identity and source. At no time is my Highest Self defined by external circumstances. As Love's expression, I include the solution to every problem. As Love, I am the power which re-defines the problem. The problem does not re-define me."

Because of this healing attitude, Scott and I generally do not repeat bad news. Why give it fuel? Instead, we put our best efforts towards being part of a solution. We try to remain calm so we can listen to Love and follow Love's leadings towards healing.

Have courage to address problems

It takes courage to be alive. You may be assured that, as Love's expression, you are filled with all courage to face every situation. Love's victory is with you always.

Think about yourself as Love's healing ray of light. Don't be afraid to see what you need to heal. You can shine your light on any problem in order to dismiss the appearance of its darkness. You need not be afraid. Turn up your power wattage and don't give away your power. Stand in the Light of healing Love and be guided.

You can decide now – as you face any problem – that you already have the power, strength, and intelligence to solve it. Send your light forward. Move into the solution with your radiance and your intention to bring healing. Think of yourself, and others who may be involved, as being in a place of Love's shining.

As you do this, know that the entire problem area is receiving Love's healing light and transforming it.

Open your mind and give full permission for full healing to occur. Remind yourself that Love's healing light is more than sufficient to alter physiology, change thought patterns, purify motives, arrest fears, awaken beliefs to understanding, and bring forth safety, wellness, and healing to the situation. Love transforms.

Further, remember that Love can uplift depressed energies and offer immediate comfort, hope, inspiration, and peace where before there appeared to be the darkest place. All this can occur rapidly.

Persistence is essential

Stay on it, like a firefighter with a hose on a fire, until the fire is out. Keep projecting Love in place of the problem. Let Love heal it.

Let Love instruct those who are appointed to be part of the healing. Trust Love to deliver its healing messages to those needing it. Allow Love to move through you and guide you and others to the place of healing. Stay in your power!

Become aware if there is anything you are being instructed to do by Love to make things right. Likewise, listen if there is anything you are doing that needs to leave in order to make things right. Then allow it to leave you. Stay detached from what you just released and don't rehearse it.

Contribute all you can, through Love's instruction, to the healing. Stay constant. Be diligent. Don't give up.

An example of immediate spiritual persistence

While on a walk one day, I tripped and fell hard on concrete. I took the impact on my chest and side and it felt like I cracked some ribs. I was immediately in a lot of pain and found breathing difficult. In fact, any movement was very painful.

From the moment I fell, I started praying vehemently. Sitting there on the concrete, I declared that my true Self had never fallen and never lapsed from harmony. I didn't wait until I was home to begin this essential healing work. I reminded myself that I live in Love and everything in Love is harmonious. I insisted on recalling and declaring the divine fact that nothing collides with Love. I affirmed that my wholeness cannot be cracked or broken, but is forever complete with perfection.

This, I knew, was healing me. If, however, I had stopped to evaluate the moment, I might have appeared to be a person who was suffering because I had fallen hard and was injured. Yet I was already claiming healing as my divine and natural state of being. Do you see the value of spiritual persistence from the very beginning of a healing? My husband, who was with me, was totally supportive and spiritually held the space with me for healing.

During the next week, rising from sitting or lying positions was difficult. Every time I moved, I turned to Love for comfort and instruction for the movement. It helped a great deal. Movements were restrictive. I had to avoid even slightly leaning forward. Reaching down for anything was impossible. Yet I knew Love was healing me as I continued my healing declarations. I was able to manage being wherever I needed to be, although moving slowly and with great care.

I knew that it was not the fall, but what I was telling myself about the fall that would determine the speed and quality of my healing. I also knew that it was my primary job as shepherd of the healing to herd the majority of my thoughts towards affirming my wholeness versus my injury. Outweighing the negative thoughts (which affirm the problem) with spiritual thoughts (which acknowledge healing), is always essential to spiritual healing. The sooner you accomplish this, the sooner you are healed. Listen to Love for how to do this.

My prayers in this healing were ongoing and sincere. In fact, I was in final edits of this book at the time of the fall. Happily, I was aware of how many of the teachings in this book I was applying to this healing. These healing principles have been carved out of many years of practical experience of listening to Love.

Every day, I learn something more about healing. I actually enjoyed living so closely to Love, having to be reminded of my need for Love many times each hour and even during the nights. I rejoiced that healing was taking place.

Why did I think that I was being healed? After all, I was still in a lot of pain. First of all, there was clear healing evidence of slight improvement every single day. And I knew the power of prayer. Although I had fear, I rested in great confidence that healing progress was taking place. I knew the power of spiritual persistence.

Within two weeks, the healing was complete. I was back in yoga, stretching and fully bending without any sensation or discomfort. I relied completely on Love for this healing. This is a good example of how persistence wins.

Spiritual healing is not a method of *willing* yourself to be healed. Persistence in prayer is very different than healing through will. When I think of healing through will, I think of someone who is not necessarily praying or using any spirituality for their healing. Human will power can be dangerous in healing. Anytime we have a problem and don't listen to Love for guidance, we have placed ourselves outside of Love's healing range. When we listen to Love, however, we discover that Love is always available to us every moment, if we will ask.

Who's in charge?

You and Love are the determining factor in every situation in your life. The problem is not the determining factor over you. Love is the only cause and power. Occupy your Highest Self at all times and do not abandon yourself. Feel the authority of divine Love infusing you with healing power at all times.

Remember, if you do not daily define *who* you are and *how* you are, it will be done involuntarily for you. Take an active role in your right to be happy, strong, well, and free. Stay in your divine power and don't give it away. Let us now add even more power to our understanding of spiritual healing.

The next chapter will teach you how to make tidal wave affirmations and denials that dissolve obstacles with Love.

Chapter 11

Tidal Wave
Affirmations & Denials

Energy follows thought.

Consider the fact that your mind thinks about 100,000 thoughts a day.

What percent of your thoughts each day are affirmative to your health and well being? What percent of the thoughts coming to you from others are affirmative to your health and well being?

Usually, people answer these questions with a very low percentage number.

And, conversely, what percent of your thoughts are denials of Love's presence of perfection? This question causes us to see that we need to re-think almost everything.

Does this mean that Love thinks? Absolutely! Love is the consciousness of all seeing and all knowing. Love is the mind of God, the source of all intelligence. So let us think *as* Love!

Spiritual healing is more than just exchanging negative thoughts for positive ones. In spiritual healing, we utilize divine thoughts, allowing them to grow and develop our life path and life vision, while canceling false beliefs. Now there is a healing life! This is the path of spiritual healing.

How many times have you repeated and silently affirmed the following "I am" words or phrases:

- I am tired.
- I am lonely.

- I am aging.
- I am worried.
- I am probably doing something wrong.
- I don't feel loved.
- I don't want to get hurt.
- I feel unworthy.
- I am limited in my job.
- I need more money.
- I feel weak.
- I feel ill.
- I hope this prayer is working.

These are all affirmations and they tend to be self-fulfilling. We become what we most affirm. Repetitive negative affirmations recycle false beliefs and are the opposite of healing.

Surprisingly enough, when you step outside beliefs, even for a few minutes each day, and affirm what is true about yourself, based on Love's reality, you bring about healing. When Truth is introduced in place of a negative belief, healing begins.

Healing affirmations are based on what Love is saying

Begin by thinking of what Love is affirming in place of what a negative belief is affirming. For example, if your inner tape is saying, "I am afraid that I will wind up alone in my life," leave this negative belief and rise to see what Love says about it.

Would Love state that it is alone? Never. This is your first clue of which affirmation to use in place of loneliness. State it from Love's standpoint. Love would say, "I fill all space. I am with you now." And remember, Love is the authority, not the belief. This is not wishing. This is healing based on divine Truth which is supreme. All healing affirmations are based on affirming from the place of Love's reality. Love alone carries the authority and power. The lesser always yields to the greater.

Affirmations are always in the present tense

For example, if you have a problem with employment, your inner affirmations might be something like, "I need a job. I hope I can find the right job. I'm running out of money."

Your healing affirmation, however, would reach for Love's thoughts on the subject and would say something like, "As Love, I am employed continually throughout eternity. I am in my right place, doing my right activity. My actions are purposeful and useful and fulfilling my destiny. I am compensated by the universe for my right stand and actions. I am fully compensated for all my good."

Your affirmations would not say, "I am *going* to be employed. I am *going* to be in my right place. I am *going* to be purposeful and useful." These affirmations are not in the present tense. Do you see the difference?

Affirmations are not gimmicks

Affirmations are not a slick remedy to use as a convenience to by-pass listening to Love. They are not intellectual, positive words that you say hoping that they will come true. They are not an equal exchange of negative inner talk for positive inner talk.

Affirmations are also not a device to use in order to convince yourself that everything is all right so you can ignore the problem. They are not a reason for by-passing what the angels are saying. In fact, healing affirmations are what the angels *are* saying.

Affirmations move us beyond negative feelings

Negative feelings are natural in our lives. They indicate some level of hurt or suffering within us. Sometimes, we resist moving to a healing place because we want to honor the feelings we feel so deeply, even if they are negative. As important as it is to honor our hearts, we want to be alert, as healers, to moving higher.

Healing calls for us to break through resistance into Love's healing space. The best strategy for doing this is to gently convert our thinking to the process of making affirmations that take us into healing.

Affirmations replace problems

The existence of a problem is a negation of Love's reality. Let Love's healing affirmation replace the problem with the divine presence as it dawns within your consciousness.

Love's affirmations are a means for us to detach from beliefs and move right into healing. In using affirmations, we are awakening to what already exists as reality. This awakening displaces the belief.

In selecting an affirmation, be specific in identifying the problem. Use the affirmation as the exact opposite to the problem. I use lots of affirmations all day long. We want thoughts unfolding in our consciousness each day to be led by Love's healing affirmations. Be specific. And let them flow from you generously.

Examples of healing affirmations for sadness

Many calls I receive are from people experiencing sadness for different reasons. Sadness is often our first response to a negative situation. Here are few ways to apply affirmations to heal sadness.

If you are suffering from sadness, the healing affirmation can affirm the presence of Love's joy, gladness, uplift, peace, and bliss. You can precede these affirmations with "I am." Thus the affirmations may be, "As Love's presence, I am joyful, glad, uplifted, peaceful and blissful. I am filled with joy. I live in a state of completeness and light. I flow with exuberant happiness!"

You may protest, "Yes, but, I don't feel that way!" Of course you don't, at least not yet. But affirmations are a means to step outside your state of confinement and awaken to your Highest Self.

If the sadness is caused by separation from a loved one, here are some specific Love affirmations. "As the expression of Love, I am one with all Love. I can never be separated from Love. Love and I are one. Love is present and fully companioning me every moment. Thank you, Love, for being with me always and making your loving, healing presence known to me. I trust that You manifest in an infinite number of ways throughout the day. Thank you that I am always loved and complete with Love."

If the sadness is from disappointment, you may affirm, "I am filled with Love's strength of joy. Every thought in me is brimming with joy. I am removed from beliefs of disappointment and personal outlining of how things or people should be or the way I wish they were. I am learning wonderful lessons of wisdom and I am grateful that I can exchange personal disappointment for Love's outline, which is always perfect. I am filled with forgiveness to myself and everyone. I accept that Love has a better plan than I thought that I needed. I accept that all things are perfect right now."

A healing affirmation addresses the false belief and all that accompanies it. If there is depression, continue to persist with your powerful affirmations.

Sadness and depression have a tendency to be prolonged since they argue for themselves. This means you are going to become an expert at filling yourself with thoughts and affirmations which are full of Love's divine, healing joy as you release the negative. Let your affirmations intelligently open doors of joy for you, reveal why you suffer, show you what you can do about it, and guide you through it step by step. Affirmations are powerful to bring about healing.

For example, I knew a woman who had decades of depression in her life. In overcoming it through healing prayer, she discovered that she had buried herself in comparisons of herself with her very dynamic, successful older sister. Her healing resulted in her becoming one of the most joyous persons I ever met. Her inner peace was unshakeable. In fact, she told me that, even if her house burned down with everything in it and she was standing outside at night in her nightgown, watching it burn, it could not take away her joy.

Love's affirmations help us to develop the practice of living in sustained Love reality.

The best affirmation is your own, from Love, not someone else's. If my affirmations help you, please use them. But more importantly, listen to Love for your own specific affirmations. This is about your own relationship with Love, not mine. Love has millions of healing messages for you every moment. As you listen, you will flow with them and you will see healing results. Stay with it.

Using a worksheet to make healing affirmations

When I give a healing treatment, I often work from a worksheet. I always have a writing pad close by. Here is what I do.

Using a blank page, I draw a line down the page, dividing it about one third on the left and about two thirds on the right.

On the left, at the top, I head the one third portion as "Beliefs." And on the right hand, at the top, I head the two thirds portion as "Love's Reality."

Returning to the "Beliefs" column, I list all the things that identify the problem. For example, if I feel like I'm coming down with a cold or virus I will list under the "beliefs' column all the things I want to deny as being true about me.

This will be things like: fear, contagion, consent, virus, bacteria, vulnerability, harm from others, fever, congestion and whatever else I may be experiencing. These are not the qualities of Love or Love's expression and that is precisely why I am denying them. They don't belong to me, or you, or to anyone. Note: I always begin with fear as the first denial on every treatment.

On the right side column, I then write words that indicate Love's reality. They will be the opposite quality of each denial. For example, here are some of the words or phrases you might find on my right hand side, which correspond to the beliefs:

"As the expression of Love, I am comforted, assured, strong, able, defended, shielded, unharmed, unharmable, safe, and secure. This is my total condition and I give my consent only to this healing Truth. I am pure and free of contamination. I am the activity of continual strength right where there appears to be vulnerability. My consciousness is filled with power, thwarting false beliefs, refusing to accept them as real. Every cell in my body is filled with this report of complete health, strength, and power. I know this to be true and I occupy this Truth as my own."

You can see that I am taking a stand for what I know is my right of perfect health. I have done this type of wonderful stand against all kinds of illnesses and diseases and infections with great success.

You are beginning to see the mental strength of the work in treatments. Now we will take it to the next level. Are you ready for Love's gigantic healing power?

Tidal wave affirmations

One night, I had a dream where I felt Love's powerful energies as a tidal wave of healing power. From the imprint of this Love dream came the most bold, outrageous affirmations flowing forth as a tidal wave of healing Love.

The affirmations below speak for each one of us as a tidal wave of Love, covering the universe. As you read them, think of these applying to you and awakening your Highest Self to come forward in more Love! Think of yourself as Love's tidal wave and these affirmations as your inner talk. Here they are. Remember, they are from Love and not spoken from ego. Claim these as your own.

As Love's Expression:

- I am in full power covering all that exists. I saturate the world in my love.
- Nothing can stop me.
- My momentum is immeasurable.
- I source total Love energy.
- I move at incredible speed being every-where at once.
- I affect everything in my path.
- I distribute myself everywhere massively at my all-powerful level. My love is a monumental and towering presence everywhere.
- I am beautiful, grand, and able.
- I am beyond human invention.
- I am Self-created and Self actualized.

- I am perfectly formed, amassed, and energized to be all that I am meant to be. And I am empowered to do all that I am meant to do.
- As Love's tidal wave, I am visible, credible, and covering all space with my loving presence and essence. Everyone feels my caring, compassionate essence and presence. Everyone deeply appreciates my Love presence, including myself.
- I am blessing everyone, everything, everywhere.
- I fill all space. I am filled with joy!
- I am absolutely abundant!
- I change all things. All is changed and dramatically transformed by My healing presence.
- I am Love's Highest Self.

Even more tidal wave affirmations of Love

Get a feeling for these tidal wave energies. Allow yourself to be in the experience of unlimited infinitude. See how far you can read before your inner critic begins to protest. Try to go past your set limits. You can be outrageously bold in Love! I think archangel Michael has a sense of humor! Affirm to yourself:

- I am a healing machine!
- I am a healing system that says, "All healing is within me and operating in me with full speed ahead!"
- I am projecting my healing Love to every one on earth.
- The science of my body and life is divine and supreme. This science causes me to be a self-healing system that automatically

self-cleanses, self-corrects, self-maintains, and self-sustains my state of perfect being.

- My perfection is ruling out of me all imperfection.
- All the infinite possibilities of healing are unfolding within me now.
- I am being divinely guided towards complete healing.
- I am completely open to Love's healing today.
- I am Love's powerful healing action.
- I am enabled to know everything I need to know for this healing to appear now.
- I am filled with the Light of healing!
- Absolutely nothing can prevent me from healing!
- Love and I are a divine and powerful healing presence, unfolding this healing in full.
- All that I am doing towards this healing is divinely authorized and is totally effective at once.
- There is no such thing as an incurable condition!
- Nothing is too hard for Love to heal.
- Since I am immortal, I am fresh and new each moment. Age cannot hold back my healing.
- Since I am eternal, there is no *time* to work against me in this healing.
- All advantages to healing are on my side.
- I am unlimited in my healing. Every advantage of healing is mine.
- Love empowers and enables me to experience full and complete healing.
- Love wants me healed today.

- Love enables me to know all that I need to know and learn all that I need to learn to be a total healing presence.
- Love causes me to be healed.
- This healing is taking place every moment.
- The angels won't leave me alone until I am completely healed!
- I have unlimited intelligence to know exactly and precisely how to heal.
- I understand how this healing is coming about and I accept it in full now.
- I love learning more about healing Love every day!
- I love growing spiritually! This is fun, empowering, and freeing!
- I can hardly wait to do my daily healing prayers and see what Love is telling me.
- Through prayer and meditation, I am fully connected to Love's instruction.
- My prayer and study are guided by Love and are enormously effective in healing me.
- Love pours out all that I need for this healing. Love withholds nothing that I need.
- My daily prayers and intuitions – led by Love – are totally successful. This healing is taking place!
- As the expression of God, I can see this healing occurring.
- Nothing can separate me from this healing. Love sees to it that I am healed!

Waves and waves of healing

This tidal wave dream stayed with me for a few days. Here are more of Love's wonderful yang energies for you to practice. I have been adding a few denials in the mix too. Just remember, you are practicing divine reality. This is the real you thinking:

- I represent Love which prevails over this problem.
- This problem must succumb to divine Love operating through me.
- This problem is not true, no matter how true it appears to be right now.
- This problem represents a mess. And it is not my problem or my mess!
- I represent Love, which is supreme over this belief.
- The belief is in all ways inferior to my healing Love.
- I am the expression of Love which denounces, eradicates, and nullifies this claim with total and immediate success.
- There can be no false claim about me. This would be a lie about God.
- I refuse this problem.
- I refute and deny this as a real problem.
- I have never lapsed from Love, therefore I am Love's expression, which has no problem.
- My only heritage is divine and is all good. My coding and history are Love.
- I am authorized by divine law to be Love's appearance, action, power, substance, and life to every situation calling itself a problem. I remain safe, well, and harmonious in Love.
- Love operates in me as a powerful healing influence to reveal the problem as untrue, throw it out of my experience, and nullify it once and for all.
- I am Love, which is the presence and activity of defeat to the problem.
- This belief cannot pin its erring theory on me.

- I am holding this belief in captivity.
- I disallow the darkness of this problem. In fact, my Light outshines the problem and effortlessly brings forth the most harmonious and immediate solution.
- Love is operating in me to harmoniously eject this negative experience.
- Love is repelling me away from this problem.
- Love compels me to out-picture the solution, while dismissing the problem.
- Time cannot operate as a factor in this healing. No belief of delay, labor, pressure, stress, strain, lapse of time, postponement, too late, or need for hurry can interfere with any part of this healing.
- Love – active within me – is a prevention to the problem.
- I cannot be harmed or experience loss as a result of this problem. Love ends the illusion of my having a problem.
- The problem cannot act as an extreme in my life. No belief of imbalance, severity, crises, or degree of hardship can manifest as my true experience. I am exempt from extremes and imbalances. I am forever balanced and stable in Love at all times and in all ways.
- This problem cannot define me. I am more than this problem.
- This healing treatment doesn't have the option of being ineffective.
- This healing treatment is the law to every problem that would deny, obstruct, or obscure it.
- I hereby name this problem as illegitimate and I outlaw this problem from my entire life experience and being.

Tidal wave healing denials

All problems are, in fact, a denial of Love's reality. Tidal wave healing denials reverse all impositions on Love and assert the healing Truth.

Tidal wave affirmations and denials may feel strange because we aren't accustomed to expressing ourselves so boldly. You may have resistance to being so bold because you consider this an aspect of yourself that you aren't comfortable with.

In some respects, tidal wave denials are even more bold than the affirmations. Try moving in this direction of your power and expand from your present comfort level. We are not re-inventing you with power. We are claiming the power that is inherently within you which you need for healing. You are taking back what you have forgotten or did not know.

Slowly, see if you can begin to embrace your power. Your attitude is one of defiance, as though you are indicating, "How dare anything rob me of my right of Love's reality! I am taking back what belongs to me!"

As a Love healer, your attitude is one of defiance against anything that would interrupt Love's flow in your life! This is not anger, but the Divine Power's rebuke to the problem.

As a spiritual healer, I have a mindset to triumph and prevail over any problem. My attitude is that I am here to heal, not to lose. I never give up. Never. In all our healing work, we can put pressure on the problem to conform to Love, and off of you! There are times that I *really* lay into it!

Are you feeling the attitude of strength behind healing? It is as though you, as a healer, have been assigned to go in and straighten out the record keeping. You will no longer allow illusion to write the record. You are here to make Love's correction and re-align with reality.

Often, as a spiritual healer, I feel like I am flexing my spiritual muscle. The more you flex a muscle, the stronger and more defined it becomes.

There are times that you can be galled by the problem, such as, "How dare this try to overtake me! Love and I are already on the other side of this healing as winners!"

At all times, know that Love can heal anything and everything – against all odds! Boldly resist the problem with your whole divine being!

Take a "no nonsense" approach that you and the healing are absolutely unstoppable, undefeatable, and that the healing is present and successfully operating at this and every moment!

Know that Love empowers you with all that you need and, as you tune in to Love's instruction, you and Love are the presence of total victory!

Think in terms of power words to describe you – authorized, bold, a force of divine Love, unstoppable, undefeatable, supreme, energized, strong, secure, invulnerable, uninvadable, and unshakeable!

Remember Love's Allness. Love is all present and completely available every moment. Love's Allness fills all moments and constitutes all reality. Remove the belief that denies present perfection and watch perfection appear.

It is not the words that bring healing. It's the spirit. Catch the spirit!

The following statements of denial represent my inner thinking when doing healing work. Take advantage of what it has taken years to develop that causes me to be a successful healer.

Try to crawl inside of the meaning of each of the following denials. This is also massively powerful immunization, protection, and defense for yourself and others.

Acceptance:

I won't be made to accept this problem under any condition. Nothing can influence me to be made to believe it. This problem is not my real thinking or experience.

I am not buying this problem as belonging to me. Nothing can convince me that this is my problem.

Do you see? You are throwing it off you!

Displacement:

Love acts through me to act upon the problem to displace and eradicate it.

Refusal:

I refuse this problem as part of my reality.

Attachment:

This problem cannot attach itself to me.

Projection:

This problem cannot be projected on me as a real problem. I cannot be made to be the recipient of a mental projection appearing as a real problem.

Imposition:

This problem cannot be imposed on me by anyone or any circumstance at any time.

Resistance:

I have absolutely no resistance to this healing. I am completely open to all Love's healing guidance and I am totally willing to change and go higher now.

Channel:

This problem cannot be channeled to me nor can it find any means through which it can move through me, my life, or my loved ones.

Image or Picture:

This problem cannot be imaged on me. I will not picture myself with this problem. I will not be made to have this problem pictured *on* me or *in* me.

Heredity:

My only true Source is good. All that I inherit is from Love and my inheritance is a total blessing. I release all false heritage of harm and trouble of every kind.

Subtleties:

This problem cannot come to me through any hidden, unknown, or subtle ways or means. Love's alertness and wisdom guard my thought and life always. My total well being is intact. I am alert and safe.

Force:

I cannot be made to have this problem forced on me. I cannot be made to be oppressed, suppressed, depressed, or pressed in any way. This problem cannot pressure me to feel opposed. As Love's being, I am literally unopposable.

Dis-ownership:

This problem is not mine. I won't take it on as mine. I hereby disown this problem.

Relationship:

This problem has no relationship with me. Nothing in me is related to this problem. I have no association with this problem.

Un-Believable:

This problem is unbelievable to me. I cannot be made to believe it. This problem is merely a belief. I am not a believer in beliefs. I am empowered with Love's spiritual senses, which are my only interpreters of reality. Spiritual senses cause me to override the appearance of problems and live in the realm of powerful healing Love.

Appearances:
I cannot be fooled by superficial appearances. If it is not from Love, it does not even exist. Love alone is all. Love commands this and every moment with total authority and a wonderful outcome!

Conditioning:
I am trained only by Love. Love is my only conditioning. All other conditioning is released from me. All that comes to me is of Love. All that flows out from me is from Love. Love is the all and only influence in my life, ingraining its healing presence and modifying me perfectly.

Cause:
Since Love is all that exists, there is no cause outside of Love. I rebuke the problem as a real cause. I vehemently remind myself of the one and only true Cause that blesses me and everyone, revealing its true magnificent effect.

History:
My history is eternally now. My history is Love's presence. In my history, there is nothing that could ever harm me, no matter how familiar it is or how many times it may have seemed to appear in my experience.

My only history is Love, which causes me to remember my forever being-ness as Love. Therefore, my eternal history defines me as good, innocent, pure, filled with integrity, honor, beauty, majesty, excellence, dignity, perfection, wholeness, complete-ness, and worthiness – in the family of Love, Fathered and Mothered eternally by Love.

Time:
Time is no factor in my healing. I am eternal – timeless and ageless. Every moment is the present moment of my infinite, divine Self.

Interruption:
I have never lapsed from perfection. At no time in all eternity has my harmony or perfection been invaded or interrupted.

Energy:
This problem represents energy that is not mine. It does not represent true divine energy and I disallow it. In the name of Love, I hereby repel this problem's energy.

Substance:
Since Love is all that exists – all that has ever existed, or ever will exist – Love is all true substance. My substance is Love. My substance is good. The condition of my substance is excellent at all times.

Action:
Love is the all and only action. All action is Love. My actions proceed from Love and flower into Love's manifestation.

Intelligence:
Love is the only consciousness and only source of all intelligence. Love's intelligence creates all that exists. I am the expression of Love's intelligence. Love reports its own perfect reality. This invalidates false reports that appear to be intelligent but which are based on a faulty perception of reality.

Authority:
I, as Love's expression, am authorized to override this problem. This problem is under my divine

authority and it must surrender now to Love's healing power.

Basis:

This problem has no basis whatsoever. It has no fact, no foundation, no support, and no fundamental principle of Love's reality on which to base itself. Since there is absolutely nothing to uphold this problem, the problem must collapse and fall. Note: I am not the one that must collapse and fall. It is the unreality which must collapse and fall away from my life once and for all.

Let these affirmations and denials be a model and support as you develop your own unique healing approach to defeat all beliefs challenging your well being.

In the next chapter, we will discuss empowering laws of spiritual healing to give you even more clarity on healing with Love.

Chapter 12

Empowering
Healing
Laws

Finding the right attitude is everything in spiritual healing. It is imperative to get on top of the problem and prevail with Love. I utilize healing laws to help me gain a powerful attitude to dissolve a problem.

It requires mental positioning or a mind set in order to triumph in healing. The sooner you gain your position, the more you will experience calmness, peace, and progress as the healing inevitably takes place.

Here are some laws of healing which I have discovered from my practice that are especially helpful to bring this forward. As you read these and apply them, you will learn more about your spiritual power and how to wield it.

The law of intention

The mere intention to heal something offers an immediate energy towards the solution. Intention brings focus to direct your thoughts toward healing.

As your intention remains directed towards healing, you open yourself to healing inspiration and energy.

As you set forth your intention, avoid judging the outcome. Don't listen to thoughts that question your ability to solve the problem. Keep your intention open to healing. Remember, you are not healing something real. You are merely waking up to reality, which, in turn, nullifies the problem.

The law of displacement

This may be one of my favorites. It is full of yang.

Ships have a water displacement factor. We live in San Diego where the enormous Navy ships are often docked. Some of them are over twenty stories tall.

I often think of these ships and how it must have been the first time they were lowered into the water. Can you imagine the amount of water that had to be displaced in order to make room for the mass of the ship?

I like to think of this while giving a healing treatment.

Just as the ship displaces the water, so does Love's healing reality displace the problem. See yourself as master over the problem and overriding the problem in every case, every day.

The law of overtaking

Think of movies where good overtakes evil or where the Mother ship overtakes and rescues the ship in trouble. Practice feeling this same power within you. Then wield Love's healing power to overtake the problem. Say to yourself, "This is fully my true, divine Self in action!"

Override and overtake the problem with Love's healing reality.

The law of "greater than"

Consciously think out from your Highest Self in order to experience your position of being greater than a problem. This is a healing principle and carries great power in overcoming any and every problem.

When beginning healing work, a problem appears large and the solution appears small, even remote. It is a dominion factor. What is dominant? Problem or solution? Good or bad? Highest Self or the problem?

Make the bold assumption that, at the onset of any problem, the healing is already present and is the dominant factor. No matter what the problem is, how bad it appears, or how aggressive or involved it is, your Highest Self is already carrying the perfect solution and is greater than the problem.

This deals directly with perception. The healer's attitude is to reduce the perception of a problem as large, while viewing the solution as present and far greater than the problem.

How? By listening to Love's healing solution.

In spiritual healing, assumption is essential. Here is your sustaining assumption. You are greater than any problem, and all problems combined, including the greatest challenge presently facing you.

Remember where to place your trust and faith. Love's Allness is the fact that precludes the belief of any problem being actual. I prove this every day in my healing practice and so can you.

The law of imprints

Thoughts that become enlarged create your immediate reality. They make an imprint. If you think about something negative over a period of time, even briefly, you will soon come to believe the negative and it will, most likely, appear somewhere in your life – in your body, your relationships, your emotions, your bank account, or your dreams. It may appear as an irritation that you can't shake.

It's the law of imprinting.

On the other hand, if you focus on Love's healing reality for a several days, you will soon come to see things that once challenged you as less a problem or no longer a problem. You have offered a new imprint to replace the false imprint.

Here are some examples of imprints. If you spend a morning with a car mechanic discussing problems with your car engine, you will carry that around in your consciousness in large measure that day. You will assume that these are your thoughts and this is your reality. It is a mental imprint.

Likewise, an unhappy relationship creates bad feelings and negative interchanges which imprint your life with unhappiness. This is a negative mental imprint and needs to be addressed and healed.

We are continually imprinting, making mental impressions which we take in. It is, therefore, important to take initiative and keep the mental impressions of Love ongoing in your consciousness, singing your song, and not allowing negative images to drown it out.

For example, guess what kind of a day you will have and what the main imprint will be that leads your day if you:

- Wake up in the morning and immediately Identify your Highest Self,
- Take time in the shower to listen to Love and be meditative,
- Read something spiritually inspirational, and
- Speak and act with loving-kindness throughout the day.

Our daily imprints play back to us in repetition. In order to go forward and progress spiritually, we need to maintain a dominant spiritual factor throughout our days. This can be done easily and with little effort, but consistency is the key.

Turning your thought to Love many times throughout the day and evening, and opening to Love's healing messages, act as powerful preventive medicine as well as a strong and happy way to live.

The law of attraction

When I consider some of the most severe cases I've witnessed, I see the false law of attraction at work.

Life has many ups and downs. Let's talk about the downs from Love's stand-point. There is absolutely no place in your life, no matter how bad it gets, where healing is outside of you. You have the ability, at all times and under all circumstances, to attract an immediate solution to you.

The immediate solution may not be the long term solution. But you are headed for the final solution even in step one. Don't judge the solution. It may not be the one you personally picked out. I am often surprised how Love solves problems. Trust Love to guide you. I am often amazed, looking back, at how a healing took place and how impossible it would have been for me to have figured out or known Love's solution.

Please know that the law of attraction is always working in your behalf, attracting all the thoughts, images, help, people, and turn of events in favor of a right solution.

I have often thought how Love will turn the universe upside down in order to arrange a perfect outcome. Love has the big picture. Trust Love's healing law of attraction to attract exactly the right mate, children, events, job, place to live, life purpose, support, opportunities, and fulfillments for your greatest benefit. Trust Love to attract all that is necessary for your greatest benefit including attracting you to right inner thoughts and motives, intuitions, spiritual understanding, and the ability to express love, joy, and holiness.

This, of course, does not excuse you from making rational and wise decisions or from taking active human steps to manage your life with intelligence.

I recently heard a news story that beautifully illustrates the law of attraction.

In the middle of the ocean, a Navy man fell off his ship. His ship mates did not know he had been separated from the ship. In the great waters, there was no apparent help for miles and miles. He was a tiny speck in the vast sea. The picture was a bleak one. But the news story went on to report that a hospital ship, called The Comforter, came along the exact same path and spotted him in distress. Though he had been struggling for his life for over seventeen hours all alone, and no one knew his whereabouts, the divine law of attraction was at work and saved him.

The news reported that he had been praying through the many hours.

The law of Mother Love

This is the law that ends fear. We realize Mother Love and its power to transform suffering by its presence and energy of calm, comfort, quiet, soothing peace, blessing, unity, understanding, compassion, and deep caring.

Whether you are male or female, it doesn't matter. Mother Love is present equally within us, because Mother Love is all present, always.

This is not a contest between father and mother and who is more valuable. They are equally valuable. The yin energies of Mother Love are the first comfort we receive in healing and are indispensable to healing. Mother Love is so welcomed!

Have the goal that, when people come into your healing atmosphere, they are greeted with Love's calmness, comfort, compassion, and peace. Above all, bless others with your Mother Love and contribute this enormous healing presence to the universe so in need.

This does not mean that you are always serious. Laughter, playfulness, and joy are equally healing and comforting.

The law of Father Love

Again, whether you are male or female, it does not matter. We each have equal proportions of this invaluable law, always operating in our behalf. It is innate within each of us.

Father Love is yang. It oversees healings and stays strong in overriding false beliefs. Its strength and power are always with you to draw from generously. Rely on Father Love when you need courage, strength, resources, supply, momentum, progress, and defense. Turn to it when you need to feel that something so much bigger is working to bring forth healing to your greatest advantage.

The law of Love's Oneness and Allness

Consider the fact that there cannot be two things that exist at the same time in the same place. There can only be One presence. Love's reality is the only presence, everywhere, and at all times.

Love is a "single" presence. Although Love has infinite individuality, without duplication, it is still One.

Often we relate through dualism. There's your opinion and there's my opinion. We seem to be in disagreement. Yet Love is always in full agreement with Itself. In Truth, there is no duality. Love is One. Love's unity never fights or is in conflict. Love never says, "I am in disagreement or conflict with myself." Love's Allness is always in complete agreement with Itself. This is the healing Truth.

Consider this. Would Love hurt itself? Never. Then, in Truth, you can never be hurt if you are Love's expression of Oneness.

Love constitutes all being – all thought, all action, all interpretation, all understanding, all intelligence, all truth, all presence, everywhere, always, and all at once. Love is the healer of heartbreak, loss, illness, conflict, crime, violence, and war. Love's Oneness and Allness precludes all problems.

Love is the One Self. All self exists as this One Self. The one Self has one Mind. In reality, each of us has only one consciousness, or Mind. It is the mind of God.

When you practice thinking from the consciousness of Love, you are thinking in Love's Oneness. This is the Consciousness that heals everything.

Love is indivisible. It cannot be divided. Love's purpose never separates, but is forever unified.

Looking out from Love's vision, we see our wholeness and perfection, infinitely, and all at once. At no point does Love see variance from its perfection. At no time does Love say, "This part of Me is good, but this part is not." Nor does Love think, "This part of me is separated from Me," because Love is All that exists.

Love is without a moment of division from Itself. When you are thinking as Love's Consciousness, you see that you cannot be broken, torn, cut, separated, excluded, or experience any loss whatsoever. It is impossible for Love to separate from Its state of perfect being. You are the expression of Love's Allness. This law of Allness is forever operating to your greatest advantage. This is your law for healing all division.

The law of immunization against illness

Let me tell you the secret of immunization. It is to put up a strong defense, sufficient to protect yourself from harm.

I have practiced the law of immunization as my physical health care program for almost thirty years, without using any medicine. And Scott has practiced an entire lifetime of healthy defense without medicine. I have also used the law of immunization in toxic relationships as well as on the freeway in times of danger, and whenever I feel vulnerable within a relationship, or have feelings of any loss. Since this law is so important to your well being, I will go into full detail.

Whether harm is coming from a toxic relationship, abuse, unfairness, violence, a virus, bacteria, contagion, disease, or vulnerability to an accident, you need to be aware of the need and opportunity to actively and consciously keep yourself safe and defended at all times. Children need to be taught this as well. This work is prayerful and mental.

Let's discuss this law as it applies to physical health. Mental alertness is vital to your defense. For example, every winter when the pharmaceutical companies wage an aggressive campaign to convince us through advertising that it is "flu season," it is time to come to your defense right then and there and prevent yourself from being under mental attack. If Scott and I are watching TV, we immediately hit the mute button, not allowing it in – even the visuals.

The same is true when people are discussing symptoms of illness in social conversations. In such settings, Scott or I may say something comforting, but we will gently and lovingly change the subject – unless the person is asking us for healing support. It is surprising how insistent people will sometimes be in rehearsing their symptoms. As a healer, this is a call to action. Whenever I hear symptoms, I cannot leave them alone. I am always active in neutralizing such thinking in my consciousness.

Scott & I also do not read articles discussing illness or disease or their symptoms. We spend our time reading loads of uplifting spiritual works, which keep our consciousness filled with spirituality.

I believe that each of us is actually safer in a room full of people with highly infectious diseases than in a room full of people who are *discussing symptoms* of infectious diseases. People have no idea how totally mental the belief of contagion is, and how readily we give our mental consent.

We tend to give our consent every time we fear contagion or think we have a symptom of something believed to be contagious. Yet we can remove our consent by simply denying the problem and replacing the fear and symptoms with the truth about our real, divine self. Divinity heals.

Some people think that the denial of symptoms is enough. It is not. Mental exchanges of symptoms for spiritual truths are necessary to remove and replace the problem in consciousness. We out-picture what we most hold in our thinking.

Unfortunately, we are slowly allowing the pharmaceutical companies to create a new calendar, making us believe that nature is harmful to us and we ourselves are catching harm from each other. Our consent to this only adds to the problem, creating it as a reality for everyone. Do not give your mental consent to allow yourself to become brainwashed into accepting that you are vulnerable to attack. Just think, if everyone quit believing false beliefs, we would cease to see them manifest in our lives!

Let's also discuss "allergy season." Please let your oneness challenge the belief that you could be allergic to anything. Would any part of Love's Highest Self react unfavorably to another part of Love's

Highest Self? Never. Nature is in harmony with all of life. I have seen the successful healing of poisonous spider bites as well as poison ivy by knowing and affirming that Love never created poison. Practice seeing yourself as completely invulnerable. And practice the view that all creation is harmless.

There is always a latest finding about something in our environment that is toxic to our health. If we stand ready always to agree, we are merely adding to the problem and opening ourselves to its symptoms. This is the way false beliefs become ingrained. Contagion is mental. If you apply the law of Love's immunization, you will find much of the power of healing through your refusal to agree with the false beliefs. We can, in fact, resist all contagion, even the latest findings.

When you are in an elevator and someone is coughing, sneezing, or blowing a nose, it is time to be alert and shield yourself, and them too. How? By knowing that you and this person are the presence of Love and what you are catching is the presence of Love, not germs. Love brings no harm whatsoever. Picture it. Hold to your picture. Make it stick.

Practice affirming to yourself, "As Love, I do not give my consent to illness."

It is helpful to be specific in your mental treatment. For example, if one of the symptoms is congestion, first identify it as a belief. This may be hard for you since it may seem so actual at the time. Nevertheless, the identification of a problem as a belief is the first step towards healing it.

Then sufficiently counter the false belief with it's healing opposite. For congestion, for example, I often use the image of Love flowing as a pure river with all its channels wide open, free, and unobstructed. This may be my anchor point for the entire day, thinking of it many times throughout the day.

For infection, you can counter it specifically with the reminder that you are spiritual, divine, and therefore invulnerable and shielded at all times. You have never lapsed from perfection in Love's kingdom. This, of course, is more than mere words. The counter to any problem comes from both logic and divine inspiration. What is Love telling you? Ask Love. Then listen. Then affirm.

If Love is all that really exists, what are we catching? Love. How could we catch anything but Love if Love is all that exists? We cannot. How can we have any condition other than Love if that is truly who we are? This is not mere pie-in-the-sky theory.

Here is where metaphysics offers scientific proof. This is not merely a theory about Love. Proof follows the divine facts whenever these facts are applied diligently. I see the proof of the law of defense constantly in my healing practice, where people call me with descriptions of a cold, flu, virus, infection, congestion, sore throat, fever, ear ache, and inflammation. Then they are healed by the truths that I am sharing with you.

Practice this law of healing when the thought comes of being under attack from chemical, biological, or nuclear warfare. These are all equally false beliefs.

Does an illusion suddenly become a reality because it seems to be vehement or aggressive? No. Never.

These symptoms are not true about Love and they are not true about you. They are also not true about anyone else. There can be no condition outside of Love if Love is all there is. See the application of your oneness with Love?

Consistency of spiritual thought is everything in spiritual healing.

It's easy to know your spiritual identity when the sun is shining and you feel healthy and loved. But when problems come, it is even more important to know your spiritual identity, because it is your defense against harm.

Immunization is a divine law blessing you at all times. As you come into remembrance of your natural state of defense as Love's own, you begin to experience the healing effects of this defense.

Your mental and prayerful stand sends a new report to every cell and throughout your entire system. The body will follow the report that is most powerful and which most prevails in your thought. Since vulnerability is not a divine fact or law, it succumbs to the divine law which then prevails over the place of vulnerability.

You are in charge of the report in your body. The report is not in charge of you. This is your healing attitude. You are having an effect on the problem and the problem is not having an effect on you. Keep reminding yourself of what is true. This spiritual work is not tiring you but strengthening you.

Your oneness with Love means that there is not even the tiniest area where anything other than Love can be present.

Your age does not matter. Love rules. Start now by practicing this and your practice will cause you to realize the power of healing yourself.

When symptoms come, state and re-state your case of invulnerability thoroughly to yourself until the fear of contagion and symptoms leaves you and your inner peace is restored. Unfortunately, we have been trained to believe we are fragile, frail, and vulnerable, subject to attack at any moment, and a helpless victim to circumstances out of our control.

Since so many people believe in contagion, I find that speaking against contagion out loud in conversations in favor of our defense and our right of freedom from illness usually only complicates matters. In such cases, let this be between you and God, or you and someone who has the same understanding as you and can hold the healing space with you.

When visiting a sick friend, it is time to know that the love that brings you there also keeps you safe and brings them healing. A cup of love is far more potent than a cup of chicken soup. If you bring the soup, please also bring the love! Caring love brings us protection, not vulnerability.

Mother Teresa did her life work for decades among the diseased. She is a wonderful example of personal immunization. It was not a miracle but a divine law of defense that she exercised by her clear understanding of God's love being present and operating in behalf of her charitable work.

When I find myself coming down with symptoms of illness, I begin at that moment resisting the thoughts of symptoms. I wage a counter attack on the belief and I am aggressive. I will not practice vulnerability to illness or disease in my thought. Usually, by successfully denying it and affirming that I am of Love, and therefore am invulnerable and inviolable, all mental rehearsal of the symptoms and physical symptoms leave. Love is supporting you. Persistence is vital.

There may be periods when it is so aggressive that I cannot shake it for a few days. During this period, however, it rarely moves into something full blown such as fever and illness. I stay on it like a fireman with a hose to the fire. I won't stop my treatment under any circumstances, until I am free.

I may need to address it repeatedly dozens of times in a period of a few hours, seeing myself as strong, invulnerable, invincible, protected, safe, and fully empowered against attacks. During these times, I continually see myself spiritually. It only takes a moment to do this, but it is well worth it.

If it is necessary for me to do this repeatedly for several hours, I find that, by keeping these thoughts as my background music, I can also do healing work for others as well. My hours of holding the space open for my healing will pay off and either the symptoms will leave, or the aggression of the thought of them will be greatly reduced. I continue working until the last thought is challenged and gone. It does little good to take an aggressive stand for your immunization only to back down later.

The work of seeing yourself as Love is the same no matter what illness appears. Know that you are not a victim. You, as Love, are victorious and triumphant, always.

If the symptoms are visible, avoid looking in the mirror as this tends to instill it more in our thought – since we tend to believe what we see. Try to avoid checking to see if you are healed. Remember who you are and see yourself, instead, as filled with and covered in Love's pure light. Keep the pressure on the belief until it yields.

It is helpful to avoid tracking down how you got it, where you got it, and why you got it. When those thoughts come, just remind yourself, "That is not me." And if, in fact, you have a lesson to learn from it, Love will unfold that harmoniously for you. Love's law of immunization says that you are uncontaminated.

Know that you need not get worse before you get better. Don't think of yourself as waiting for the healing. Expect full healing every moment. Love is that good to you! Love takes you all the way, not partially.

You deserve to be healed. You are worthy of healing. Throw out all guilt.

Remind yourself that you are the precious expression of pure Love. Embrace yourself and your healing as the will of Love. It is Love's divine will that you are free of illness, physical problems, and disease.

Every time you think these simple healing truths, you are bringing forth the energy that reinforces and fortifies your healing. Healing is not something you are trying to gain. Healing is what you are awakening to already within you.

Think of your healing as present and operating within you. This presence comes with a plan to heal you. It is fully equipped and enabled to be 100% successful. Allow the healing to take hold of you and integrate itself fully with you. Cheer it on!

Consider the alternative of not taking a stand for your defense and winding up in bed ill. The few moments of taking powerful stands for the right of your health and well being can save you many days and weeks from suffering in bed.

In the last fifteen years, I recall only two or three times when I needed to go to bed with an illness. In all but one of these times, I was up and free in less than twenty four hours, because I continued to pray and vehemently hold my spiritual stand between naps.

When I am around people who are coming down with something – the cashier at the grocery store, the parking lot attendant, a friend, family member, or loved one – I am alert to having healing thoughts about them, as well as myself. If I think, "I hope I don't catch that too!," I recognize it as a fearful thought, a vulnerable thought, not one of my thoughts. Instead, I think of them as Love's expression, pure and free, and completely defended from attack. I bless them and all those around them, knowing Love is operating as their full defense. I envision them catching love and healing from me.

When reminding ourselves of our protection and powerful defense, we do not become tense, afraid, or stressed. Spiritual work is calm, confident, and peaceful, full of Love's presence and assurance. You are merely recalling what is absolutely true for yourself and everyone else so you do not fall into the trap of believing you are subject to any condition of harm.

I recently asked a client what she thought of when she imaged divine immunization. She told me she thought of Michelangelo's statue of David. She marveled that David stood there relaxed and peaceful having come from slaying the giant Goliath. She said she felt God gave her that inspired insight as she viewed the masterpiece in Italy.

We reasoned together that here is a young, victorious, valiant warrior who has just emerged from the battle of his life, not with a puffed up chest of pride, sweat, flexed muscles, or exhaustion, but with calmness, peace, and serenity. This is our confidence too. We can feel calm, cool, and collected when doing our spiritual work. Love is with us all the way, guiding our healing safely home in calm victory.

Each of us is immunized from harm. We may need to take action at times to be wise and stay alert, but the divine law of defense can protect us in every case whenever we draw upon it. Preventive medicine works.

We need to come into greater understanding of our permanent state of invulnerability, and practice the unwavering stand that healing is our right and we will prevail. Love is with you all the way. Draw strength and power from this law that protects you always. And be willing to take practical steps in your behalf.

For example, if I feel like I am getting a cold, I need to not be around people who are discussing this or agreeing that there is something going around. This may also not be the time to visit a friend who is ill. Take care of yourself first. Then you can tend to others.

Take a look at your Highest Self. View its invincible power and strength. Think of yourself as a fortress, impregnable against attack, safe under every circumstance. Think of the fact that there is no invention that can possibly alter Love and its permanent condition of wellness and wholeness.

Nothing can enter Love to harm or destroy. You and Love are one. You are Love's invulnerable, immunized, empowered tower of strength and might. Nothing can harm you.

This applies equally when you feel vulnerable, including times of low self esteem, inadequacy, loss, depression, or any negativity about yourself. We need to practice the law of defense every single day so that we can live from our highest point of who we truly are.

In the next chapter, we will discuss the all important healing of toxic relationships.

Chapter 13

Toxic Relationships & Healing

Toxic relationships often create physical problems that hide, in the most subtle ways, the healing we deserve.

We suffer physically, for example, from allowing people to treat us in condemning ways. Few people see it. Few people realize it until it has become so severe that, through much prayer, the reason for their physical suffering and pain slowly dawns on them.

Just as our bodies have a constitution, strong and fit, or not, so also our emotions have a constitution. When the emotions are allowed to be in pain time and again, we do not know what to do with the hurt and so it becomes stored in our bodies. The hurt becomes toxic to our health and well being.

When someone calls about a physical problem and I offer a treatment or two and it does not improve, I often surmise that there is a toxic relationship involved. I speak from my boldest and most honest place of transparency. I want you to get this. It could save your life.

Open your eyes

Pull back from your life right now and take a look at the big picture. Of all your relationships, which one or ones cause you pain?

We are reluctant to admit that our sons' and daughters' neglectful or disrespectful treatment of us causes us pain. We are hesitant to admit that our spouses, life partners, moms, dads, friends, bosses, or fellow workers are causing us pain. But this is the place I am asking you to survey at this moment. Let's go there together now with Love and have healing.

Thank you for trusting me with this very tender area that we build many fences around in order to avoid thinking about. I assure you that Love is right here as we view the relationships that are closest to your heart.

Sometimes, at our Love Center workshops, I show the depth of the toxic things we suffer from, headed under the column of beliefs. The list is long. It has words like: condemnation, accusation, hurt, harm, blame, ridicule, criticism, disrespect, demeaning, manipulation, and name calling. Does this sound familiar to you?

The effect of these behaviors is toxic. They cut deep and they send inner messages to us of guilt, unworthiness, fear, loss, despair, and finally, depression. We feel like a failure. See the deepening of the wound? We don't know how to fix it. We quickly deal with it by storing it away. What else can we do? We store it away adding hurt and anger. These two, left unhealed, have long-term negative effects on the body.

For most of my patients, these healings take a long time simply because they can't believe the problem is from how they allow someone close to them to treat them in a negative manner. Once they get it, however, the healing comes forth.

Unfortunately, people often suffer from hatred from loved ones. This is a very hard one to see because it is emotionally confusing. After all, they say they love you. And they are the ones you call family, you count on, who know you best. You assume they could not harm you and you know they would not willingly do such a thing.

Nevertheless, it is just as toxic, especially long term, as slowly drinking a bottle of poison, causing great pain, suffering, and sometimes even death. A number of people have told me they would be dead today had we not done our healing work together on their toxic relationships. Yet, at the time we worked together, they protested that it was only a physical condition since they didn't see the real problem being from a relationship.

Confusion perpetuates the problem

In family or close relationships, we are accustomed to keeping in touch, especially at important times such as birthdays, holidays, vacations, weekends, good times, and hard times. We count on them. We count on the intimacy. We call this love.

Often, unfortunately, we are willing to put up with their occasional insults, their habits of inserting their opinions of what we are doing wrong, and their criticism. When we allow this to undermine our decisions and inner confidence, we lower our opinion of ourselves and our ability to be resilient. Our self-esteem sinks.

This sends a message to our bodies that we are not able to defend ourselves and our bodies are vulnerable to attack, just like our lives.

It is amazing how we become conditioned to tolerate or accept this treatment for ourselves. We may not like it, but we are resigned that this is the way it is and we cannot change it. They have convinced us. Their poor treatment towards us dominates.

People who practice abuse have subtle ways of creating guilt. We feel the effects but we rarely see it unless we are alert. Ironically, the abusive person often blames the innocent person for the very thing that the abuser did wrong or failed to do. For whatever reason, the abuser gives himself or herself justified permission to let loose on the innocent person. Innocent people are caught off guard. Attempts to defend themselves are also blocked and disallowed. Do you see a pattern here?

Innocent people think, in response, that they themselves can change and do better in order to please the other person. This is not the way to stop harmful treatment.

Basically, we become dominated by the gall of people who think it is their right to judge us. Is it their right to judge you? Did anyone check with you on giving this right? Does this sound like divine Love?

What I most hear in response about now is, "But I've told them over and over and I have protested being treated in this way." Yes, I know. And they still haven't changed their way of treating you. They continue to justify that they are right and you are wrong. Your voice is nullified. What you say does not count. There's the conditioning. There's the problem.

How do they get by with this behavior?

You think you are somehow obligated to allow them to judge you. And you judge yourself as wrong for even thinking or questioning that they are wrong in their treatment of you. They say, however, that they are not judging you and that *you* are wrong.

This is the person whom you claim to love and who claims to love you. You think maybe you are somehow partly to blame. You feel ashamed for the mess. You assume responsibility for their failure to love you. You can't shirk their bad advice, criticism, or negative judgments. You need to feel better, but how?

You are reluctant to move them away from your inner heart. You tell yourself, "Maybe I need them." You tell yourself that losing them would be worse than keeping them. Maybe it's better just to keep them, just in case. After all, there aren't that many people you are close to and you do need intimacy.

Positive intimacy causes you to feel validated, valuable, and worthy of love. It opens the heart. Perhaps, you reason, negative emotional intimacy is better than having no intimacy, even if it often closes your heart. Basically, you have decided that a certain amount of domination is better than no domination. You compromise.

That's how it happens. See the web?

Awakening to this with clarity is powerful preventive medicine. See it now. Stop it before it goes further.

Take a look at your relationships. Which ones need to end? Which ones can you work with and expect a turnaround within a short time? Be honest.

Here is your first clue. There is hope if the other person has a truly loving, compassionate heart, and not sometimes, but pretty much all the time. This means that they are willing to change bad habits. There is also hope if this person is on the same path as you, the path of personal growth and not just saying they are, but making changes and making honest effort to live a spiritual life. The relationship also needs a spirit of cooperation and helpfulness. Be honest in your assessment. This is an all-important decision in managing your life happiness and well being.

We act out scripts

Here I am, a family person, a child, a mother, a dad, a single person, or a business person and I am getting up in the morning, walking through my day with the belief that:

My (love mate, parent, best friend, boss, etc.) keeps telling me I am wrong. "Maybe it's true," I say to myself. "They make me feel that I am wrong. As a result, I feel guilty, even though I don't agree with why they think I am wrong."

Then the tapes play throughout the day, though now in a new way. The tapes don't say "you." They internalize the condemnation and play it back with inner talk like: "I don't feel adequate. I don't feel valuable or necessary. I may not be able to cope well today. I feel vulnerable. I may not be protected on the freeway, on the playground, or against my boss."

The inner talk says: "I feel helpless, ineffective, unempowered, disadvantaged, vulnerable, separated from harmony, struggling, alone, out of control, struck, beaten down, and defeated. I feel it is useless to even try to overcome this."

What do you think is the effect on the body?

Set new standards and take healing action

Don't let your love be bought cheap. Set standards for yourself by having people in your life who have mutually-shared values. This is a case of managing your life by managing the choice of your relationships. This may mean an immediate change for you.

In *Liberating Your Magnificence*, a healing book co-authored by Scott and me, we have an entire chapter called "Surround Yourself with People who Honor You." There has to be a place where you are willing to draw the line and take a stand for what you deserve. The attitude needs to be, "Now is the moment I take this stand for loving myself."

I am not suggesting that you react to the person or persons with anything harsh, angry, lashing out, or severe rebuke. I am suggesting, however, that you become aware that, whenever you are in relationship with people who do not live according to spiritual values, this presents a challenge. Rather than enabling the problem to continue, let Love help you do something about it. Begin now.

You can decide, for example, to have a loving, open conversation with the loved one who condemns or judges you and share how you feel in their presence.

In this conversation, you want to avoid saying things like, "You hurt me. You did this to me!" You want to be the one who sets the most loving tone. Speak from your own inner heart. Begin by telling them the top three things you most appreciate about them. Let them know sincerely what their value has been to you.

Then tell them that you have been doing some very deep thinking. You have become aware that there are areas in your relationship that cause you to feel hurt. Be specific. Tell a story. Help them to understand.

Don't lose your temper. Keep it objective. If there are a few times or many, let them know that this has been repetitious and that the hurt has gone deeper every time. Thank them for listening. Ask them to help you end your suffering.

Tell them you are sorry for the difficulty. You know they never meant to hurt you. And you certainly have not wanted to hurt them or be hurt by them. Nevertheless, this is what has happened.

Perhaps they will be able to discuss it right then. If not, ask them when they may be able to respond to your call for their help. Indicate that your heart needs an answer.

This may be the first time in your relationship with them where you will be revealing the standard that they need to come to in order to stay in your inner circle. Hold the line. Let there be silence. Don't cover for them. Don't excuse them or yourself. Don't accept guilt for what they have created. Don't let them off the hook. Let them be uncomfortable, if needed, in order for them to reach for a higher place. Don't apologize for their wrong doing.

If this leads to a conversation where you realize you have also wronged them – we're often ignorant of our actions and their effects – then thank them for pointing it out. Let them know that you will give this great thought and prayer.

You can offer sincere apology for your own actions if you agree that you have wronged them.

But if your loved one is defensive and angry in response, give him or her time to cool down and think it over. End the conversation and excuse yourself, saying you want to give them time to think over the things you have said. Do it with love. Let them know you love them and you are trying to prevent yourself from being hurt anymore. Be encouraging that you have faith that things can change for the better so you can both be equally happy.

If their final response is to make you wrong and they continue repeating their old hurtful behavior, then you have your answer. Take action. Lovingly tell them that you have an obligation to yourself to have in your life only the people who are loving and caring to you, who are compassionate about defending you, and who avoid hurting you. Share with them – and yourself – that you want a life of love, harmony, mutual compassion, praise, and positive intimacy.

Explain that this is how you define standards of love for yourself. Let them know that, if they change their mind about their treatment of you, to let you know. Do not excuse bad behavior. Excuses enable it to continue. Don't be an enabler.

If they tell you they have decided to change their behavior, give them another opportunity to redeem themselves. But don't go to sleep. Hold them accountable. So often, we take a stand in a heated moment and our life partner, family member, business partners, or friend knows we'll back down when the heat is off. Hold the line for yourself. It's up to you.

Loving yourself within close relationships often requires great finesse. In some cases of toxic treatment, and after honest attempts for healing with no improvement, you may need to separate. In other cases, you can keep love flowing to your family yet protect your heart from abuse.

For example, if you know already that your life dreams or living choices will be criticized, judged, or condemned, learn to keep your sacred life steps to yourself and share them only with those who honor you and your life direction. This requires a tender balance of love for yourself and love for others.

Be highly selective in who surrounds you. Make sure they are equal to your lovingness. Make sure you do not allow yourself to be mistreated. Do not accept their word when they protest and defensively react saying you are the one to blame, unless you truly believe it is so.

This isn't about ego. This isn't about who is right and who is wrong. This is about being at peace with your Highest Self and getting on with the life you deserve, managing it with the best decisions possible so your suffering ends and your happiness soars. You have no obligation to anyone to allow yourself to suffer in pain, hurt, or anger. Make a new decision and make it today.

Read *The Love You Deserve, A Spiritual Guide to Genuine Love* by Scott and me. Our lives are devoted to educating people about the genuine love they truly deserve.

Do all that is necessary to consider your happiness and the happiness of your children, if they are involved. Consider what you are modeling to the children about how you deserve to be treated. Otherwise, they will learn from your life partner what is appropriate.

I have seen some of the loveliest women accept abuse from their husbands or sweethearts, and when their children grew up, the children treated these moms exactly the way they saw modeled to them by their abusive or disrespectful dads or mom's sweethearts. Exceptions are rare. This is preventable. Take charge of your relationships and make sure you are treated with respect and dignity at all times and by everyone around you.

Refuse to allow yourself to be treated in a way that causes you to be unhappy. Speak up, even though someone may disagree with you. You alone are in charge of your life. Do not allow yourself to be trampled. It is your spiritual right to be free and maintain freedom from toxic relationships.

Forgive yourself. Offer yourself full cleansing and forgiveness for associating with one who continually brings you down. Do not be responsible for their poor behavior. Accept no shame. Realize that evil (or someone's ignorance) cannot stop you from going forward with your beautiful, pure Love light. It is time for you to shine, shine, shine. Love is calling you.

The principle of Love needs to be upheld. Remember what genuine love looks and feels like. Love is kind, honoring, supportive, understanding, caring, compassionate, fair, just, and honest – consistently. It takes a lot of work to show up with love for others. Expect this from yourself and from all who surround you. Love is a tall order and is admirable because it requires the discipline of constant practice. Violating Love's principle or overlooking it is pure indulgence. If you indulge someone's harmful behavior to you, you are out of Love alignment. Do not wonder why your emotional or physical body hurts.

Develop courage to take right action in defense of your right to be well loved and your right to flow with positive feelings with those closest to you – so that you can be free to flow with generous love to them. This doesn't happen when our hearts have to close due to hurt and when we feel emotionally unsafe. End high maintenance relationships. Do not be afraid.

Scott and I have no high maintenance relationships left and we live in indescribable, endless harmony that is truly heaven on earth. Our innermost relationships support our life, help us to stay encouraged, and cause us to believe in ourselves that we can do the work that we feel we most want to contribute to the universe. How important is that! We do the same for them too.

The cost of hurt and anger

I have seen the effects of toxic relationships on the body and it is not pleasant. It shows up as chronic pain, infections, and disease. I have had patients tell me they wanted to die.

When you fail to defend yourself, the body goes into the same mode. It loses its defense and immunization. It sends a message of vulnerability. The body duplicates what is going on in your life and in your heart. What we think and how we allow ourselves to be treated eventually effects our health.

Consider the cost of failing to speak up, allowing your voice to be drowned out and your feelings to be invalidated by another who tells you that you are wrong in your decisions, goals, actions, or overall way of conducting your life and relationships.

Consider what is at stake.

Your life mission deserves massive support

Your life is wide open to reach its greatest potential. You are on a mission. Your work is God-appointed. Your Soul has purpose and direction. You need massive support. Other Souls need massive support, understanding, care, encouragement, help, and tender compassion. Now this is what our relationships are for – mutual Soul building!

If you want to find your Soul mate, you first must be on your Soul path. You will not be on your Soul path as long as you are using all your energies to unsuccessfully defend yourself, retreat, live in fear of saying or doing the wrong thing, or being intimidated by those who think it is their right to dominate you. All your energies will be used to defend yourself.

Learn to be a voice for Love. Lovingly speak out against what creates hurt. Disallow it in your life. Effectively defend yourself and help others do this for themselves as well. Listen for Love's angels for direction and let Love prevail in standing for principle, not indulgence.

Lean on angels to guide you with wisdom and grace and keep you from harm. Remain strong in your stand for what is right for you.

Forgiveness is divine

When we have done all we know, and said all there is to say, and there is still no change in someone who causes us pain, suffering, and hardship, the finest thing you can do is to forgive.

This does not mean you keep such people in your life when they do not change. In such circumstances, you don't keep them. Your health can't afford it. There clearly needs to be a distance between them and you if they care so little that you suffer because of their poor treatment of you.

Let me tell you what forgiveness is not for. It is not to condone the wrong done to you, and it is not to excuse it or to send a message that they can do it again. Forgiveness does not mean that you will become a door mat, vulnerable to being walked over.

Forgiveness is what you can do to dissolve your bad feelings. Forgiveness is for you to have peace in your heart. You need forgiveness in order to put away hurt once and for all. Remember your loving nature.

There are times that the person you need to have a conversation with, in order to try to straighten things out, is no longer available to you. They may have moved or even passed away. How, then, do you make peace with the wrong done to you?

I know of no other way than to forgive. There is no better time than the present, even if the hurt was created years ago.

In fact, I try to stay current with forgiveness because I want to stay close to Love at all times and I am not willing to give away my peace to another person. Forgiveness is, sometimes, the only way to resolve and heal issues.

Otherwise you mull it over, have the conversation mentally where you are setting things straight with them, and this occurs over and over without any end in sight.

Sometimes we hold on to anger when we have been wronged, and we use anger as a defense to feel safe and protected. This is not helpful and will never lead to healing. This is not a healthy defense, nor is it strong. Holding in anger is never to your advantage, especially as a defense system. Neither is venting anger helpful. That only harms others. Anger needs to be addressed and healed.

I have seen the faces of people who cannot forgive or refuse to forgive. Over time, they have faces of stress, deep lines, and frowns. Their faces do not reveal inner peace. Resentment creates knots and even disease. You do not need to show the person how much they hurt you. We do not need to play the hurt heart game of "See what you did to me!" This is off the path of Love and it only perpetuates anger and hurt.

We do not need to seek pay back. Love is strong and revenge is weak. Remember who you are and, at all times, act from your Highest Self. This is to your greatest health and well being.

It is not about them deserving your forgiveness. It is about your own right to live with a peaceful heart, free of anger, hate, revenge, and resentment. Forgiveness is for you.

Forgiveness is powerful medicine for the body. It does not re-open the door to recreate the problem. Forgiveness allows you to deal with the hurt up front, name it, offer yourself comfort and solace, and then put it away in peace.

On things difficult to forgive, you will have to practice forgiving it every time it comes to your thought, until the pattern is changed and hurt no longer comes up for you. Forgiveness does not allow a quick fix where you do not deal with your hurt and, instead, you ignore it and sweep it under the rug.

Ask Love to show you how to forgive all the wrong done against you. Be patient with yourself and keep making the effort, while listening to Love, until you succeed. Then the mental images that torment you and keep you in anger, hurt, and disturbance will no longer appear.

You have a right to live in peace and Oneness. This is who you are. You can disallow anything and everything from separating you from Love. You are on a mission and you have work to do in order to fulfill your purpose. Forgiveness releases you to go forward. Be a witness to knowing that this same truth is true for everyone else as well.

Let forgiveness flow and feel the healing!

Chapter 14

Your Life Purpose & Abundance

Most of the world's population struggles with the need for a sense of life fulfillment and adequate financial supply.

How does Love heal in these two critical areas of well being?

Simply stated, your healing premise is this: all your abundant supply and life fulfillment come from Love. In Love, we find our true life purpose and all our needs are met.

This is a very bold stand, entirely outside the box of limitation that we generally accept as reality. This means that beliefs of limitation, lack, loss, scarcity, and inadequacy are outlawed as beliefs which fail to describe the all presence of Love and its abundant reality.

Rather than viewing the challenge of scarcity as a burden, we can see it as an opportunity to see God in infinite, practical ways every day. Our lives then open with purpose and abundance.

Your niche in eternity may not be your occupation

There is absolutely nothing wrong with being a carpenter when, deep inside, you feel more like a minister. This means that you are in the ministry of carpentry at this moment. This does not say that you will never become a minister.

My husband is clearly appointed by Love to teach love's standards and skills and to counsel with Love, yet he still sells real estate. Guess what? He doesn't wait until real estate hours are over and then put on his Love suit! He acts out his authentic Love self all the time and from there his life takes shape. This attitude has enabled him to also write books and articles, teach love, and co-direct TheLoveCenter.

The only real questions are, "What is your Soul saying? What is your Soul doing?" Don't let your occupation or world standards of success identify who you are. Let Soul do it by its spiritual standards. Let's talk about this more.

How visible are you?

Here is a question I often ask people. How visible are you? On a scale between 1 and 10 (10 being the most), how would you rate your visibility? How many people really know you and know what is in your inner heart?

Most people answer with a 6 or below. One woman answered with a -20! Happily, during the workshop, she moved right up to a 10. And you can too! The good news is that you are the one in charge of revealing yourself. No one can do this for you.

The reason we don't come out of hiding is simple. We are scared. It is risky. We may lose love from those close to us, or we may lose love from those considering loving us. We fear that if people really knew us, they may not like us so we better not be too visible. We fear that what we perceive as our inadequacies and unworthiness will be found out.

There are other reasons we resist being visible. We reason that, by becoming visible, people might have information that could be used against us. Or people may be jealous and gossip to others about us if we step out too visibly. We may also risk rejection.

We fear that by becoming visible, we may possibly fail and then everyone would see us fail.

Consider what happens when people become visible at a 10, revealing who they are and openly sharing their gifts. Monet was at a 10 when he painted the water lilies. Handel was at a 10 when he wrote the Messiah.

Others through history have courageously stepped forth into their life passion and left their legacy, enriching us all. You don't have to be a martyr like Gandhi or Martin Luther King or be saint-like as Mother Teresa. Oprah is at a 10. Olympic winners are 10's.

In fact, you know 10's. They are not common, but you know them by their enormous inspiration, courage, boldness, and light. They are around you. They are people who have courageously taken the risk of rejection and the fear of being known and they have stepped forth to be all they could be. We love 10's!

Revealing yourself at a 10 does not mean spilling your sacred beans or that you need to tell private information about yourself that deserves to be confidential. For example, Monet shined at a 10 without our needing to know his personal matters.

Can you really afford not to step up and be all you are meant to be?

Your identity signature

Each of us has a Soul signature. It is what you hold in your heart with great desire to enact in your life with deep meaning. Soul is a description of your core. It makes you who you are and causes each of us to be unduplicatable. It needs to be identified. The more clearly we understand ourselves, the less vulnerable we are to others' mistaken, subjective descriptions of us that cause us to suffer. And also, the more clear you are about who you truly are, the more attention you can focus on it and nourish it to come forward even more.

I recall one afternoon at the park while Scott and I were sitting on the grass, reading. I was deep in thought and wondering what my Soul Self, or Highest Self, looked like. I prayed.

A burst of enormous inspiration came forth and I put down the book I was reading. I turned to Scott, saying, "Would you like to see what I look like inside me and view my true identity – my Soul?" He eagerly said "Yes!"

I stood up. Using my arms, I described myself as an enormous body of water moving forward with massive Love energy and momentum.

I continued to act it out. Looking behind me, all I could see was more water. More of this fantastic powerful energy was moving forward through me as a tidal wave of Love healing.

I overflow and gush my healing Love waters, spilling over lavishly. It felt deeply satisfying to act it out, using my arms outstretched in front of me to cover everything in my Love and to dissolve all suffering. I spill and splash Love everywhere! I was on to something huge here! This was beginning to feel very familiar! This is what I do as a healer. In fact, I often feel like a powerful waterfall, spilling with healing force and power. This is my Soul identity.

Then I asked Scott to show me his identity signature at a 10.

He was a little self conscious, since people were milling around the park. I asked him "If you won't show the world your Soul now, when will you do it?" He took me up on it and soon focused on his Soul. Then he began to act it out.

Opening his arms, he looked like he was embracing and then hugging the entire universe. He said this is what he does. He embraces everyone with love. Then his hands reached forward, palms up. He explained that he was supporting everyone in his love. His hands then moved upward as he released everyone to Love's Light. He ended with his hands in the pose of "namaste," an ancient word from India meaning (approximately), "the divinity within me salutes the divinity within you." You can see this namaste pose faintly pictured on this book's cover. This is Scott's identity signature. Isn't it beautiful?

I felt like I had just seen God.

These are us at a 10. This is our Soul's full visibility.

I asked Scott, as I now ask many people, "How long have you been doing this?" His answer was, "As long as I can remember." I hear this same answer over and over. The invisible Soul self has been within us, enacting itself over and over. It's been with us all along.

Yet one of the hardest things we ever have to do is to be our real selves – uncondensed, unconforming, not needing to please, and untimid. You, too, have an identity signature. As you read on, let Love begin to move you towards it. Open your heart to your Soul self.

Let me tell you about Hannah, my six year old friend. Her grandmother, Georgia, came back from one of our Love Center workshops where she learned her identity signature. As Georgia showed her daughter, Michaela, her identity signature, little Hannah (Michaela's daughter) was watching. Much to the surprise and delight of the other two women, Hannah asked if she could show them her identity signature, too.

Right before Georgia's and Michaela's eyes, little Hannah began her Soul's performance. She walked over to each of them and motioned her hand towards their hearts. She said she was taking all the bad thoughts and hurt from each person's heart. She continued to act out the removal of problems from people's hearts as though there were others present. This is what Hannah is doing with her life!

Then she explained that she was placing all the bad thoughts that hurt people on a cloud, high up, which then was blown away forever by a wind. Hannah revealed her inner heart's longing. This is the explanation of what she most cares about, what she lives to do, what she enacts over and over. She is a compassionate, caring heart. This is her God-Self. So beautiful! Hannah visible at a 10.

At workshops, people have revealed their wonderful identity signatures – and they are all unique.

One man stood with his arms moving slowly up and down from his sides. He stood tall. He was a lighthouse. He said that his Soul's light saves people from storms and leads them to safety. How healing!

A woman stood with her hands overhead, straight up in the air. We asked her to please tell us what her Soul was doing. As a flame, she said that her fire is two-fold. First of all, it lights the way for others. Second, it purifies by its fire.

Some people act out a sacred symbol such as bowing in holy surrender. Some act out their Soul by placing their hands together in prayer or to express reverence through the namaste pose.

I have a friend whose Soul exudes stability. She is both buoyant and stable. I've seen her in stressful times, in times of grief, in times of transition, and still she is the mount of unshakeable, balanced, steadfastness and endurance. I call her Mount Everest.

Sometimes I think of her God Presence when I am praying for someone who is feeling emotionally unstable. I think of my friend's divinity and I draw from it as a model of what my troubled patient also includes by divine heritage. Our identity signatures are powerful to heal each other.

Remember, at the core of every spiritual healing lies the question, "Who are you?"

Sometimes in workshops, once everyone has worked out a first rendition of their identity signature, I ask some of the participants to come on the stage and share with everyone. When I see someone who has really found their identity signature, I ask if there is anyone in the audience who needs to be blessed. I ask that person to come up too.

Then, facing each other, the person who has worked out an identity signature does it whole-heartedly with passion and a full, loving heart to the person with a struggle. There are always tears and healing that follow this.

Some people begin their identity signature by planting their feet firmly on the floor, one at a time, before they continue doing something more with their bodies. They explain that they pause to anchor themselves in prayer or stillness as they tune into God before proceeding to do their Soul work. It is often followed by arms moving outstretched to others, with great Love.

A room full of people doing their identity signatures looks like a heavenly ballet, with arms slowly rising and heads bowing and hands moving in lovely motion. The facial expressions are the sweetest you ever saw.

As each person has an opportunity to explain in detail what his or her movements mean, it brings tears to everyone's eyes. We are on sacred ground. Our Souls are speaking. What could be more beautiful than our inner hearts revealed, scripted by Love, our true purpose visible and known?

Many times, I feel like I am in the ministry of revealing God. I look for each person's God self, because I want to see God revealed. I know it is there. I bid it to come out. It needs to feel it is in a safe place to be revealed, to quietly become known. I want to see God, everywhere, all the time. Don't you too?

Uncovering your identity signature

Let's move now towards uncovering your own identity signature, your God self. Please know that it is Love that guides this all-important work.

Think of what is in your innermost heart – the passion that longs to express or act out its greatest love. What is your love doing? Stand up, place the book down, and act it out. Listen for Love to show you as you stand there.

I recently showed my identity signature to a client who came for an appointment. I shared many of the things that I have shared with you. I asked her to stand up and show me hers. I then sat down.

She stood up with a bewildered look, as though she wanted to tell me that she did not know what to do. I kept holding open the spiritual space for her to come forward. In moments, she began acting it out.

She bent forward slightly and placed her hand over her eyebrow like a soft salute. Looking out to a far away distance, she moved her body from left to right. Her gaze fixed ahead as though she was looking at something far off and away from her. She explained that she was viewing everyone and everything in her life.

Then she brought some of these people that she was viewing toward her and held them in her hands as she continued to view them tenderly, up close.

As she held them, she said she was listening to God for the highest interpretation of the people – to explain them to her.

She brought the people to her heart to embrace them and released them to the world, transformed. Tears filled my eyes. I felt as though I was in the presence of a healer. I have known her for two years and never knew this about her.

I asked her how many people knew this about her. She said only me. I felt deeply privileged. But she assured me that others would know as she practiced it each day, being her true self, acting out her Soul. She wanted her Soul to become known and to be visible to others. She was ready and eager to come forward.

Scott and I sometimes greet and part from each other with our identity signatures. It is our deepest core Soul selves blessing each other at the most powerful level.

Your identity signature is sacred. It is from God to you. It is who you are, your life work, mission, purpose, and divine identity.

The value of your identity signature

Each of us want and need to be with our Soul partner and Soul mates. We long to be with "our" people – those who have come to do their ministry here on earth. This is not for exclusion. This is for inclusion, in order to bring forth more light on earth.

Yet, if everyone is hiding at a 5 or 6 visibility, how are we to find each other? It won't happen. Finding your Soul mates and Soul community is not magic. It is a question of your inner discovery of who you are at the core level, your God self. This needs to be revealed to you, acted out, and set into motion.

Once this occurs, you can expect to attract at this level, be recognized by other Soul selves, and inspire and encourage others by your boldness, courage, and willingness to come forward. You are on your way to being a 10. Your full shine is like a lighthouse for others, to attract them and let them know that God's purpose is being enacted and honored by you. This is your spiritual work.

Can you imagine the effect on the universe of doing this? Can you imagine the loss to the universe from not doing this? Wouldn't you like to see more visibility of God? How will we see Oneness until we act it out?

You are being called forth to shine

We live in a time of danger. There could never be enough soldiers or police on earth to keep everyone safe and secure. We are in a global crises in many respects.

Never before has the world been in greater need of Love Lights, like you, to shine and bring forth a new age of enlightenment and peace. We need to raise a civilization that is trained to turn to Love and heal with Love. We need an entirely new way of living in response to what we now face.

Our planet and its species need immediate help. A new kind of help. Not a response with more weapons and soldiers but a response with Love's power and healing. Prayer and living as Love is our only answer.

We need to teach our children what love looks like, to practice more sacredness each day in everyday situations, and to turn to Love in a million ways for help. Love can save us. Love has a plan. That is why we are here.

Love Lights, like you, are being called forth into the Light to shine, unite together, offer encouragement and support, and bring forth complete healing to the planet.

Love Lights shine into the dark places and bring light – cleansing and healing. Love Lights help each other stay on the path, remembering all that is at stake, helping each other to hold the sacred space, and helping each other to prevent being brought down by belittlement, abuse, and negativity, which require recovery time.

It is time to move into your Light even more. It doesn't matter what your occupation is. You are commissioned to "do your shine" wherever you are and whoever you are with. Project your love. Claim blessings for the planet and for everyone.

Shine your healing love, caring, and compassion on the world. There are people suffering. Open your heart and send them your love! Live from your heart and your love. This is your life work. Be the person who gives a radiant glow on earth.

Trust that your beautiful, divinely-guided Light is on purpose, in its right place and activity, and on a divinely directed path. Hold your position. Realize you are a God Presence.

Let your dynamic God Presence prevail, blanketing the earth and all humanity with your enormous, endless love and care. Respond to every living thing with compassion. Prevail over all with your healing Love.

Imprint your love both near you and also to the farthest places on earth. In the darkest corners of consciousness, where people have lost their way, let your beautiful, healing Love-shine bring them back and win them over because they find Love irresistibly calling them to their God self.

Let all tears on the planet be comforted and dried. Let every heart be mended. Let hope and faith be restored. Let Love feed every heart and every mouth. Let us all gather together to listen to Love, turn to each other with Love's healing light, and shine on each other with Love's blessing. Let us act as a family of Soul.

Let us include all who live under tyranny, in refugee camps, in destitution, enslavement, war zones, ghettos, and those who are poor and without hope. Include all who live in the apathy of luxury, comfort, extravagance, greed, and waste.

Our love is more than big enough to encompass them all. You are a God Presence who is calling forth others' God Presence. Together we awaken. This is the plan.

Let us infuse every one – including all humanity, plants, animals, the earth and its air, waters, and resources – with a tidal wave of healing Love, encompassing all. Let us bring all into the heart of Love! May all be healed. May all receive the great blessing of our hearts which flow with desire to comfort and awaken!

May each of us witness the God self in each other, seeing God as visible, present, and available.

This is what life purpose looks like and this is true abundance. It's not about your occupation. Life purpose is about your identity – knowing and living your core Soul self.

Let's look now even deeper together into the true nature of supply.

The truth about money and supply

We need to think of supply and money in a new way. The problem of supply can be solved permanently by viewing Love as the answer, since Love is unlimited with infinite resources. These rich resources are available to each of us, continually.

Issues of money bring up a great deal of fear for most people. False beliefs say that we must struggle, sweat, worry, and still we will not have enough money or supply. We wish we could end the pain and burden of worry. Debt adds to the heavy load.

Where is Love in all this? Or we could ask, "Where is the solution to all this? What is Love's true state of supply?"

Love's view

Love sees that it is impossible to have or be more. Love says, "In my infinity, I am enough and I have enough, forever." Love sees its plenteousness and bounty everywhere and all the time. There is no doubt to Love that it will never run out of supply. Love's state of abundance is assured for all eternity.

Love effortlessly multiplies itself through the unfolding of its ideas. Love sees the activity of its brilliant ideas unfolding and coming together, attracting each other with intelligent purpose.

In times when I feel less abundant and in need of more money, I ask myself, "How many of Love's ideas do I include at this moment?" The answer, of course, is, "I include all of Love's ideas at this and every moment!"

Then I focus attention towards listening for these unfolding ideas while allowing them to identify themselves to me. I trust these ideas to supply me and they always do.

Where does Love's supply end? Where does it stop? There are no boundaries and there is no end. This is the vision of infinity. This is the vision of Love's rich abundance. This is your rich heritage. Practice this all important view of your abundant supply as you allow this true view to replace the fears and worries of a limited view of your supply.

You deserve success

Of course you are deserving and worthy. That is Love's view of each of us.

In the human experience, when a job is needed, our worth and value are suddenly on the line. We ask ourselves:

"Is there room for me? Will the world open up and allow a space for me to occupy? Am I needed? Will I be received or will I be left on the outside, wanting to enter? Am I qualified? Too old? Too ugly?"

Our ability to be supplied is at stake. We feel tempted to be ashamed until the world nods its head and lets us in or until we prove ourselves in the world's eyes to be deserving of success.

Yet, in true reality, this is not the case. We need not act this out. This is a belief that scripts you to take your cue and act out scarcity. You have a choice. Scarcity and unworthiness are impositions on your Soul. You are divinely authorized to decline the script. It is not you.

When you decline the script of lack, loss, and limitation, you do so for all humanity. Full abundance for all is essential for our oneness to emerge. Abundance is our ultimate, collective destiny.

Love's practicality

Love is practical. We cannot sit on our couch and say, "I am divine Love and I am attracting abundance." There are angel instructions telling you practical things to do. Be guided and do them. Ask Love now what to do. Ask Love to reveal its ideas to you.

There is a danger of quitting your job and thinking the universe will and should support your mission. It doesn't work that way. You must first prove it little by little, step by step. Love is guiding you with practical wisdom as you go forth learning the responsibilities of this all important subject of supply.

Let go of your opinion of what the universe should do for you and also your zesty will to go for all or nothing. Don't quit your day job until you have really done your inner work on this all important subject.

Keep your feet on the ground and practice the practicality of common sense and wisdom. While you are doing this, contemplate the truth about abundance and the fact that your mission is completely supported by Love. And, yes, there is a divine plan unfolding. Let it take deep root in your consciousness as you apply the truths and slowly close the gap between the belief of scarcity and the truth of your abundance.

Let changes come from within and as a result of your applications of truth. Transformation cannot be forced through blind will or by ignoring wisdom.

Think of Love Itself as your employer. Lovingly ask your employer, "Love, what would you like me to know or do right now?" Be inspired to act on the direction you receive. Keep holding the space open whenever you ask Love for guidance and persist until Love unfolds the answer in a way that is perfectly clear to you.

While you are being guided on your life path and also for your supply, know that Love is supporting, providing, and supplying you continually in ways you may not understand at the moment. Stay open to Love. Let Love lead you with practical wisdom and simple steps. Try not to outline or judge.

Scott's healing of supply

The need for supply is often met in unexpected ways. In Scott's life, for example, he yearned to be lifted out of real estate. He had always looked at this occupation as something temporary. Real estate did not capture what his Soul longed for, and it also failed to satisfy the deeper longing to be more meaningful to all humanity. The words "frustration and enslavement" often described how he felt, carrying this around every day in his burdened heart. He often wondered, through the many years of prayers, how would Love ever solve this?

Heading into his 13th year of real estate, something happened that changed the long held belief of this being a problem. Scott began the practice of yoga. Little did he know that this was part of Love's plan to solve his problem.

Through what became a daily yoga practice, Scott learned the power of surrender. It felt wonderful and was deeply healing. His practice of yoga became a practice of life surrender. His inner feelings began to change dramatically. Rather than carrying around the old feelings of frustration and hopelessness about ever getting out of real estate, he found himself able to let go of these negative feelings more and more.

Fighting within was replaced with detachment from the problem, observation without judgment, and surrender. This is the yoga model he followed.

Each time he felt the old negative feelings about real estate, he released these feelings and became an observer without judging himself. In this open space, he was able to move towards surrender and let Love open up a solution.

He felt lighter about his life and real estate occupation. He felt less defined by real estate. He was bigger than an occupation.

This led to much more happiness in real estate even though this was still his occupation. Surrendering also deepened his desire to offer Love counseling to others. He started Saturday night Love Practice sessions, open for all to come.

Detachment, observation, and surrender also brought forth Scott's passion and hobby as a photographer as a new, emerging profession.

How could surrendering do all this? He quit trying to force things to happen. His energy shifted from force to surrender and to being far more interested in Love's unfolding plan. He was learning about himself through observing himself without attachment to outcome. His energy became more meditative. He created pauses and more open spaces. He was on a powerful, yet gentle learning curve.

Before this, he thought that the only way to rid himself of the nagging feelings he had about real estate was to get out of real estate. This was the outcome he continually expected as a result of his prayers. Yet Love didn't bring the healing in this way. Love often surprises us! Rather than telling Love what to heal and how to do it, Scott surrendered to Love's plan for him.

There was no one single turning point in this healing. The combination of collective forces were at work in his consciousness through our many prayers and treatments. Scott continually worked on focusing on his substance rather than the forms of his life. Interestingly enough, his physical form effortlessly dropped about 10 pounds during this time.

Yoga acted as a catalyst to cause these spiritual forces to come into play. So did the deep metaphysics and prayers we shared with each other every day.

Today, Scott is a much happier person. This abundant supply is a lovely example of true wealth and riches. It has also led to a new freedom in his consciousness resulting in more real estate sales with many happy customers who have become good friends. Scott has been able to benefit and support clients in many loving ways.

Who would have expected real estate to also be a key part of Scott's Love practice? This shows the deep inner workings of how Love supplies us with abundance.

Essential points of supply

Here are some essential points to embrace and apply for your transformation. Remember that your divine Source is unlimited, infinite, available, and present. Loss is impossible to Love and therefore impossible to you. All things are working together in your behalf at all times. This is Love's healing plan for your blessing of abundance.

Love has pre-qualified you for your supply for all eternity. You wear Love's badge of "deserving." Love's blessing of abundance for you is unstoppable as long as you are listening to Love, open to receiving it, and following it.

As Love's own, you hold the false beliefs of limitation in total subjection to Love's law of unlimited, effortless, available, and present fullness of abundance.

You deserve fair compensation. You also deserve to be treated fairly. This is the way Love's abundance works.

Love also causes you to have wisdom, intelligence, temperance with spending, and charitable generosity within your means. It takes great discipline to practice the skills of temperance in order to avoid excessive debt and overspending. This generally takes continual watching and adjusting. As Love's own, you naturally have the purity of honesty and integrity and the power of balance and restraint.

Integrity, in fact, is essential to your abundance. Your promised word needs to be impeccable with honesty and truth. Your actions need to be fair to others as well as yourself. Honesty often requires personal sacrifice. I have found that by being honest, if I lose something in the short run, I will gain it back and more in the long run – perhaps in a different way. Never fear to be honest. This is the law of Love and you come under all Love's law of blessing when you are honest and honoring of others' rights.

As Love's precious one, you are worthy, valuable, appointed, chosen, and available to receive all the wealth of the kingdom. It may surprise you to know how the wealth of the kingdom unfolds in your every day experience. As spiritual workers, we expect miracles and we wouldn't think of limiting Love.

Love's outcome

You might hope that Love will send you a large check in the mail. Love has many ways to reveal its plan of abundance. It may be different than a large check. It may be better, but not necessarily what *you* think or would outline for yourself.

Remain open to Love's way of unfolding your supply and expect to manifest it globally. Include the universe in your prayers of supply. Their good is also your good and your good is also their good. Their good never takes from your good. When they have good, it is also yours. Rejoice that good is being evidenced in your experience, regardless of who receives it.

There is a divine law of equality which causes a constant balance of supply and demand. We are all part of the great system of Love's supply of balance.

Let Love's abundant ideas manifest to you in your daily experience in Love's wise, practical ways. There is plenty for you and for all. No one in the kingdom of Love needs to scramble for the good as though it were limited to a few.

Our plates are full. Our cups overflow. We hold within our hearts the spirit of abundance and all supply for all time. Let this begin to out-picture from your lovely, abundant consciousness.

Divine ideas produce supply

Consider that Love's infinite ideas are the true currency of your supply. As you listen for these divine ideas of supply, they bring all that is necessary for the ideas to flourish. They bring an intelligent plan, support, creativity, ability to attract others, ability to perform successfully, and ability to be recognized and named as necessary and precious. Give these marvelous ideas full credit for every capacity to initiate, produce, provide, fulfill, satisfy, and bless you and all others.

Affirming Love's supply

When I was pregnant, my ex-husband and I were down to our last $67 in the bank. Our rent was due and we were both out of work. We needed divine ideas!

For three days, I sat on the couch considering all that I knew about Love's provision of supply which I affirmed was available to us always, even when we didn't see it.

During my holy contemplation, led by Love, things were working in the background which led us to a great sum of money.

A relative called offering my ex-husband the opportunity to handle a real estate transaction. The relative had suddenly thought of the idea of calling us to handle it.

The transaction went smoothly and swiftly, offering us enough commission for many months to come. That's how easily supply can appear.

In actual reality, supply was already there. The awakening of my consciousness to its presence caused it to appear.

If you are presently suffering from limited finances, this is a specific problem you can counter with affirmations. "I flow with Love's infinite supply of generous, outpouring abundance. My abundance of supply is incapable of lapsing, loss, or limitation."

In addition, you want to address and counter what surrounds the belief of scarcity with an affirmation such as:

"As Love's expression of abundance, I am filled with Love's success and dignity. There is no shame that can enter my being or describe me. I am not a failure. I am Love's total success, unfolding eternally with abundant supply and resources. Nothing will change this. I am joyful and I see Love's successful plan of infinite and unlimited abundance unfolding in my life each moment. I release false beliefs of pride and ego because they cannot define me. I am defined by my Highest Self. I am on my eternal mission and my Soul is provided for eternally."

What can you expect for yourself?

Abundance brings up many images for us. One person's abundance might be the ability to have enough food, another person's to live debt free. Another person might hope to receive a million dollars and live lavishly. There is a tendency to associate the word abundance with sky-high amounts of money and things. This is not how I define a life of abundance.

Our first appreciation of abundance is to expect that we will be supplied daily with fresh food, pure water, safety, sanitation, and shelter. Beyond this wonderful, not-to-be-taken-for-granted abundance, we expect that we will have regular income sufficient for living without struggle. Expect abundance to also include the opportunity and means for you to give your gifts to the universe.

Expect to have you and your family's needs met. Expect that you may often be surprised at how this occurs. Expect that your prayers will guide you in this all important area of life. Expect to live with abundant opportunities, progress, and fulfillments. Expect prosperity to come in many unexpected ways that you yourself have not thought of nor outlined for yourself. Expect that you are never alone. Love is showing you the way of an abundant life.

Scott's and my abundance – Love trillionaires

Let me give you an example of how Scott and I view our life of abundance.

Scott and I live in a sacred sanctuary of love. Our home is small, lovely, quiet, and safe. There are beautiful flowers everywhere. We live in the abundance of perpetual harmony and peace between us. There is more than enough love, patience, understanding, and care flowing all the time both to and from each of us.

We are able to fulfill our passion of writing about love and healing in addition to our full time jobs. We are full of divine worship, purpose, and service. We have great joy. Most days, we are filled with heavenly inspiration, great conversations, and laughter. We trust Love to guide and keep us in all ways. We do not live in want. Our wants are simple and few. We do not have a stockpile of money in the bank. We are grateful that we are able to regularly pay our bills and on time. We feel prosperous!

Our offices are at home and we go out each day for a walk and lunch. We go to a yoga center several times each week and enjoy our yoga path with a loving, spiritually-minded teacher and friend.

We often attend spiritual events where we are inspired by ministers and spiritual speakers and where we meet other spiritually-minded people. Sometimes we are the speakers. Our life style is simple and spiritually rich.

We give generously and often to non-profit organizations, including our own, TheLoveCenter. We read inspiring books, meditate, pray, and seek divine guidance each day on all our decisions. We find that our spiritual pursuits are amply supported for our spiritual well being and happiness. Such abundance!

We live in great gratitude. For example, truly, if I had a nickel every time Scott or I commented on our gratitude for the love we two share, or for our home, or for the natural beauty that surrounds us, I'd be a millionaire! But I already feel like a millionaire – without the money – because I have and enjoy what I need and want. And I appreciate it fully. In fact, Scott and I often say that we are Love trillionaires!

Our love is rich with abundance because we share it with the whole world. We never take each other for granted. Our all-inclusive life includes all the world in our prayers and it offers us a life of rich giving to help others to both love themselves and to share more love. Our relationship is a healing love center for ourselves and others. Every problem is taken to the level of spiritual healing with Love. We are abundant with active, caring love!

We are happy. Our lives are rich with meaning, love, purpose, and joy. We have wonderful friends who share our spiritual values and who are also growing as we are. And we are continually meeting lovely, new people through our work.

One of the things that tops my list of abundance is all the joy we feel from our daughter's creativity and magnificent spirituality. Seeing her on a spiritual path, disciplined, and devoted to offering herself and those around her such love and healing light, is continually fulfilling for me, having always wanted her life to be its happiest. This is one of my deepest felt desires and it is abundantly satisfied.

In addition, my mom and dad have had a harmonious and happy marriage for over 63 years and we have a deeply loving relationship. I also have a loving brother and sister-in-law and their caring family.

This is our reality of abundance. Isn't it wonderful? You can rejoice with us because our abundance is also your abundance. You are deeply included in our love. All our good is your good too. We fully support your life of equal and even greater abundance!

A healing treatment for your abundant supply

We are not actually going through life trying to get money, health, and love, though it looks like it.

We are actually putting off the belief (or thoughts) that say we lack money, health, and love. In truth, we already include all this.

Begin every healing treatment with the reminder of your divine Self. Affirm that you already include the healing and you are already in the place of healing. In fact, begin by seeing yourself on the other side of the problem. Move – in advance – to the healing place. This presumption is powerful to bring forth healing.

Think of yourself as en empowered healer who is filled with the solution. This is one of your early steps in healing yourself. We are healing from the mountain top, the pinnacle of consciousness. From here, you see all your solutions pouring forth.

Be bold in all your healing assumptions. Love is successfully guiding you forward.

Stay in your core being, your highest consciousness. Allow thoughts to pour forth from this summit.

From this power point, listen to Love's healing angels telling you whatever you need to know in order to bring forth the divine fact that you are already abundantly supplied. Stay in this healing place. See yourself knowing this.

Stay open and when the arguments come, "Yes, but..." let them go. Release each one as you hold your lovely position on Love's mountain top. Love is sustaining you on the summit.

Remember that abundance is your true nature. You are merely recalling what is natural and normal for your divinity to experience.

Your spiritual power is a denial to any other power operating in your life.

The objective in healing is to stop believing the beliefs of lack, loss, limitation, burden, struggle, dismal outlook, doom, and despair. Whether this applies to a job, your health, age, or any other place of limitation, shift your thought higher as you allow yourself to detach your thought from the belief of the problem.

Be prepared to act on your angel thoughts. Regarding a job or income, you may need to make phone calls, draw up a plan, share with someone, write a letter, or follow up on an earlier conversation. It may seem small, but each day, Love is progressing you forth in your manifestation of true abundance. Stay on it.

Since you are emanating from Love's power, think of the problem as powerless, unauthorized, and weak. It is. One problem is no more real than another. All problems are beliefs. You have the power. The problem has no power. You are associated with the solution and not the problem. You have a relationship with Love, not a relationship with problems. Act with your Love authority.

Love is operating as an irresistible, compelling force of abundance with divine ideas flowing forth and unfolding through you. Feel the energy of this gushing, flowing, force of Love's power. See the profuse abundance coming forth from you!

Let loose Love's divine power to solve the problem of limitation or scarcity for you. See your divinity as a force to be reckoned with. See yourself as unstoppable, undefeatable, authorized, and unshakeable in your power.

Be a repellent to false beliefs. Beliefs operate in opposition to your nature as Love. Anger, guilt, fear, frustration, jealousy, doubt, and stress are not your identity and you don't want to carry them around or act them out. Refuse them. Move them away from you as you detach from them. They do not belong to you.

Breathe in your dignity and composure over the problem. And breathe out the dynamic Love Presence that nullifies the problem and disqualifies it as having power over you.

Remember that abundance is already within you. Drop self-pity for your hard time. Also drop resentment of your struggle. Resonate with your healing power instead. Rise in your power to display all that Love is pouring forth as ideas. Let them come through you!

Allow your presence of Love to displace the belief of lack. This weak belief must submit and yield to Love's powerful presence. Love is with you all the way.

Know that there is no one person and no group of persons who are capable of holding you back. If someone doesn't see that you are capable, let it go and proceed to the next person. Let Love lead you. Let Love tell them in advance that you are the one who Love has sent.

The problem of scarcity is dissolved in the presence of Love. Love is abundant and powerful. Allow Love to replace the belief. Love's healing light dispels, disperses, and cancels the dark shadows of thought that create the belief of scarcity which often seems so true.

If you do nothing to identify yourself as Love's divine Self, Love's offspring, the world will identify you in a finite, limited way. Unless you rise to take action and flex your spiritual muscle, you most likely will not see the power and full potential of your abundant Love Self.

To what extent is all this a choice? Completely! You can choose your state of mind and what you will manifest. You are not in the business of producing money. You are in the business of God. You can live with your needs met and hold fear and scarcity in subjection to your Highest Self.

The wake always follows the boat. If the boat is a small fishing boat, the wake is small. If it is a giant steam liner, the wake is large. Think of the boat as a thought and the wake as what the thought manifests. You have an opportunity to be a giant steam liner of Super Love Abundance! This is your wake of divine heritage. Let your Love wake be enormous! Affirm:

"Everything that is not of Love is not of me. Everything that is of Love is part of me. There is no possibility of my ever being separated from Love or from Love's superabundance."

Today is the pinnacle of who you are and what you came here to do. This is the best you so far. You have worked hard on your life. This deserves celebration! Go forth now in Love's abundance and watch as healing thoughts direct your way.

What a psychic told me

When I was 21 years old, flying as a flight attendant with Pan Am World Airways, I often went to London. Everyone knew about the psychic woman who did her business at a pub. The stories about her ability were far reaching and phenomenal.

She told me that she saw my husband and me writing, writing, writing. She saw papers everywhere. She laughed when she said it because she envisioned so many papers and so much writing.

Years later, in my thirties and early forties, a few times I thought back to what she said and wondered how she saw the vision of all the papers. A life of writing certainly did not describe my ex-husband and me.

Then in my later forties, my husband left. A year later, I met my Soul mate, Scott. A few years after that, we became writers. And, yes, we often laugh at the papers that surround us! We are always writing!

Here is the lesson. The psychic woman perceived, decades before it manifested, the abundance of writings. I included it then – decades before it materialized.

Each of us is walking around with our eternal supply of infinite abundance. Each of us already has the abundant supply we need within us. We can trust this both now and forever. This is an eternity lesson.

Welcome to infinite supply already within you!

Chapter 15

Nothing is Impossible
to Heal

By taking the stand now that nothing is impossible to heal, you invigorate your expectation that healing is not only possible, but inevitable. You are taking your side with divine Love.

This is my stand every day in the healing practice and I have seen it operate successfully for all these years, especially in times of what appeared to be grave danger.

I would like to share with you some examples from my healing practice where my stand that nothing is impossible to heal is the only thing that stood between the person and death.

A woman called one day saying that she had just received word that her son, who lived on an island, had been taken to the hospital in an emergency. We began to pray. She waited for word from people who were with him.

Then it came. She reported that the doctors said his liver was in the condition of an eighty year old alcoholic who'd been drinking for decades. Her son was only thirty. His liver was hemorrhaging out of control and there was nothing medically that could be done to help him. He was not expected to live past the hour.

I continued to pray with his mother, a deeply spiritually-grounded woman. She was wonderfully open, receptive, and listening as we shared that Love was governing her son. After we talked on the phone, we both continued our prayers.

The next day, he was still living, but barely. They still did not expect him to make it. They needed to move him to a major hospital off the island but his condition was far too fragile. We continued to pray, using many of the principles that I share with you in this book. Our inspiration was high and full. Truth kept pouring in and we applied every drop to him.

For days, we continued to receive the same report. He was not expected to live and, at any moment, they thought he would die. And for days we continued to pray, knowing his exemption from whatever was harming him.

Two weeks went by. His condition became a little less fragile and they thought he was strong enough to be moved to a large hospital for tests. His condition continued to gradually improve, though nothing was given to him for treatment other than our prayers.

I recall, in a more relaxed moment during one of the mother's calls to me, that I wanted to bring up something that continued to come to my thought a number of times since we'd started praying.

The word "bitter" came up perhaps 5 or 6 times over the period of these few weeks. The first time it came to me was after one of her early calls. Each time the word came up, I mentally reversed it, knowing this did not describe her son or his condition.

When I told her about this strange word, I asked her what she thought about it. There was silence. Then she explained to me that bitterness was a word that described him. She told me more detail about his attitude to life. He was full of bitterness. Oddly enough, she also told me that his liver was described as bitter. Then I knew that it was bitterness and not a hemorrhaging liver that was the real case we were healing. This is what Love revealed for our healing strategy.

From that point on, we strongly made every claim about his true disposition, based on Love. We went past the superficial appearance of things and dove deep into the heart of the matter. The claim was that his bitter disposition was killing him.

As we continued our prayers, we continued to rise above the medical prognosis, since God, and not a medical prognosis, was governing the case. We were two women who were standing in Love's healing light, keeping watch over Love's child, knowing that he was full of sweetness and love.

We continued to know this thoroughly, even when he was finally released from the hospital, but told that he may never work or drive again. Still in recuperation, he left the hospital and went home.

After praying a couple more weeks, I recall the mom telling me that his disposition was changing. She was seeing it by the way he was treating his wife. We were so happy!

As is the way in many cases that I treat, the mother was strong enough to continue the prayers on her own. I remember her telling me, a few months later, that he was back to work and driving. We rejoiced at the glorious power of healing we had witnessed and had the privilege of helping to bring forth.

Learn to take a stand

Your stand, first and always, is that no matter what you are faced with, it is totally possible to be healed. This is your stand and you will not give it up for anything, no matter what.

There are times in my healing work that I know I am the only living person on earth who is taking a stand for one of my patient's lives. I, alone, then accept the responsibility of knowing what is true and what is not. And I will not back down. My prayers are adamant and relentless. I will not give up. No matter what report comes in, you need never give up.

What we call miracles are the result of people holding the space open for a better, higher solution than the present one.

Learn to take a stand. Learn to maintain a stand consistently over time, no matter how long it takes. This is the key. You will not budge. That's it. You are set and your position is immoveable.

What constitutes your healing position? It is the fact that you have identified the suffering person as Love's expression, not as one who is struggling, but as one who is free and completely outside the problem. That is the correct position for healing.

This means, then, that you will disallow another description of them, such as dying, in trouble or danger, diseased, declining, helpless, vulnerable, or a victim. These things do not occur to Love and they do not occur to Love's expressions. Not ever. No exception.

This is truth from eternity that I tell you now. This truth about our true and only identity is based on divine law. And divine law prevails because it alone carries the supremacy and power necessary to cancel any and every problem.

Am I ever afraid? Yes, of course. Some of the things I hear over the phone are very frightening and I can hardly wait to get going on countering the fear and all that stands in the way of healing. Even while I counter it and protest vehemently about the misfortune of a patient, I continue to work. Work until you are at peace and the fear and threat have left your consciousness.

Do the prayers of my clients help bring forth the healing? Absolutely! I feel their prayers, too, and together we are a mighty team to act in favor of the healing.

It helps a great deal if the person you are trying to save wants to be saved. Many people are depressed and they see no way out except death. I take a strong stand that each of us has the divine right to stay here and work it out without passing on. Hopelessness is outlawed in healing.

Viewing death and dying from a healing perspective

I do not view death as a failure of healing. Even when the cure does not appear, much healing potential is still present and available. In all life transitions, death included, there is considerable opportunity for growth and healing. Transitions represent mammoth healing opportunities to open the heart and listen to Love.

Even at the point we call death, there lies the opportunity to gain something from what we think of as our most painful experience. The key is to continually ask Love for divine guidance as we receive Love's healing comfort and help.

One's best efforts to be healed should never be judged. There should be no guilt for lack of improvement. We do our very best and this is all we can do. This deserves great compassion, acknowledgment, and support. Coming to terms with a transition as large as this, we reach deep within our reserves from our practice of spirituality. Great sensitivity needs to be made towards everyone's efforts to feel better. Death transitions call for enormous love, both to ourselves, the one who passed on, and all loved ones involved. At such times, spiritual awareness is often heightened and there can be rich learning.

When people pass on in an orderly way, there is an opportunity for closure. Loved ones can say good bye, make amends, come to grips with differences, share the hardship of farewell, and forgive any wrongs. As difficult as it may be, this can be mutually deep and healing for everyone.

When someone passes on suddenly, however, loved ones are left to find closure on their own. Turning to Love for guidance is deeply comforting and helpful at these times.

Here is a healing view for the bereaved ones, who are generally overwhelmed with feelings of loss, sadness, separation, and even guilt. As healers, we can see for them their eternal state of unbroken harmony. View them as complete and full of love, even while it appears that they are vastly suffering from their lives being emptied of love and in a state of massive loss. As healers we can cover them in Love's blanket of comfort and compassion. Allow them to feel their depth of emotion and to gently come to terms with what has happened, as you view Love's gazillion angels guiding them every step of the way.

In healing your own grief, realize that your efforts to diminish your pain of sorrow do not lessen your love and care for your loved one. It means that you will continue your life in a meaningful, yet new way. Love is guiding you. Give yourself generous love, patience, comfort, and prayer for your healing transition.

Remember, things will get better. Release yourself from guilt that says, "I should or perhaps could have done something to prevent this." It is time to forgive yourself for anything you may be holding yourself accountable for. And to also forgive your departed loved one. Releasing guilt and anger are very helpful in the healing process.

The love you shared with them continues to live within you. In honoring the preciousness of your shared love, you are also continuing to celebrate them and all that they meant to you. You continue to bless each other, whether or not you are in each other's presence.

I feel certain there is life beyond what we call the human, earthly experience. Many people who were declared dead at the scene of an accident or on an operating table, and then returned from death, have reported that they saw their bodies lying there and were even able to repeat what people were saying at the time of the death. Many people, who have passed on for a brief time and then have returned, reported similar experiences of seeing a white light and being in a place of enormous love. Most of these people said they would never again fear what we term death, since they themselves experienced life outside their bodies.

Eventually each of us must pass on. This does not mean we, or anyone else for that matter, failed. I am convinced that when it is your time to go, you go. I have seen people who, though it seemed to be their time to go, rallied and bounced back in full recuperation. As a healer, I always work for life. In cases where someone is clinging to life, the struggle can present a strong desire to gain Love's guidance and receive healing comfort, whether or not the person remains here.

The pinnacle healing view of death and dying is that, in Love's reality, there is no death. Time is man made. We live in eternity, not time.

The practice of viewing each moment as an unfolding moment in your eternal existence is far more healing than believing that your life ends at a time when you leave your body. The corpse is merely the shell left behind as the departed continue on their journey. Consider that your being exists beyond the perimeter of your physical body. Our true bodies may not be the structure of flesh and bones as much as the qualities we are embodying and the values and truths we live as divine consciousness.

Transition is eternally a way of life. Perpetual change is normal and natural. Whether we are transitioning from being a toddler to being a high

school grad, from being employed one moment to
being unemployed the next, or transitioning through
awakening from one view point to another, our
Highest Self remains the same – changeless,
permanent, and eternal. I don't know who or where
we were a hundred years ago, or who or where we
will be a hundred years from now. Deep within,
however, I feel we will ultimately all see each other
and be together in Love. Every day closes this space
of separation as we awaken to see our unity in Love's
oneness.

When healing seems impossible

We are sometimes confronted with the fearful
thought, "This problem is impossible to heal."

This, then, is the very belief that most needs to be
countered. It's the belief called "Healing is
impossible." Never believe that a belief is real. And
the belief that your healing is progressing too slowly
or that your healing is stuck – these are also lies
about your true, divine self.

There are subtle beliefs that undermine faith
regarding the possibility of your success in healing.
These beliefs say:

"First of all, should I even try to heal the problem
through Love?" Secondly, "Now that I've tried and
tried and tried to heal the problem and it hasn't
yielded, should I give up?" Also, "Have I done
something wrong since the healing did not or has not
come?"

Let's have an open discussion about these
matters. Consider this as a consultation with your
spiritual healer.

When problems persist over time, the thought
comes, "When should I give up on the healing?"
Learn now that the principle of Love does not end
just because, for example, your marriage ended.
Sometimes that *is* the healing!

And the principle of Love does not end because you haven't yet found your true love mate. Consider this. There may be more work for you to do to discover yourself so you can be true to yourself and raise the standard of what you truly deserve in a loving relationship.

The principle of Love does not stop pouring forth healing because you decide to have medical intervention. It may be that your healing is to face your worst fears and overcome them. You may feel a tremendous sense of Love's care through the medical team acting in your highest behalf.

The principle of Love does not stop healing you just because you went bankrupt. It may be that what you are healing is to learn how to practice wisdom in managing money, or to learn temperance in spending, or to forgive yourself for what you cannot change. You may also be learning to identify your real value apart from materiality.

There are many lessons of humility to be learned as we move forward in our healings. Learn your lesson so that you will not have to recycle the belief at another time.

Love is still there offering you healing even in what appears to be your most desperate situation. Love's healing is always with you.

An example of healing the "impossible"

Let me share with you another example that tells me nothing is impossible to heal.

Many years ago, a young woman called me for help. She came to my office and said that she had been diagnosed with cancer of the stomach and cervix. She told me that it was in an advanced stage. Her doctor described her stomach being filled with small tumors. She was in a lot of pain.

We began visits on a regular basis. She continued to hold down a job, although she would often call me during the day, crying in pain. Together, we prayed and reasoned metaphysically. She loved hearing about God. This was the first time she had ever known spiritual healing.

Though she lost a lot of weight, she continued to make herself eat. We often spoke of Love's healing nourishment to her. Her healing came slowly. We worked over a period of two years in all.

She had been the victim of horrible treatment as a child. What she described sounded like torture and she had suffered a great deal of trauma. But she was determined to stay with the prayerful work until she was healed. I loved her determination. She would not give up, no matter how intense the pain or how frightening the symptoms. The healing took a great effort on both our parts, but full healing came forward.

Mostly, as is the case with many clients I work with who suffer from something chronic, she received a spiritual education from me during our many, constant contacts. And I also grew.

I have found that it is enormously helpful for the person I work with to also understand the premise of the healing work. They need to understand, for example, that God's love is forever with them and that they are not beyond help. They need to understand that Love wants them to be healed and has a wonderful plan for the healing.

They need to hear the Truth voiced in their behalf, in many ways, and many times. Assurance from one who holds the space for the healing is all important. I love to enlist my clients in their healings. I feel it is a time of great awakening. They can do much to facilitate their awakening by their efforts to learn, grow, and be willing to change, even dramatically, if necessary.

More healing attitudes

Throughout this book, you have seen my "no nonsense" attitude towards healing. Let me highlight some more of the attitudes I practice in healing everything with Love:

- You deserve to be healed.
- Love wants you to be happy and well.
- It is Love's divine will to have you free of problems.
- Throw out the doubt about being healed and the necessity for you to suffer.
- Accept as fact that you are deserving and worthy of the complete healing, and now.
- Time is not a factor. Know that it cannot pressure or stress you while healing is taking place.

Healing moves at the speed of your thought and your open willingness. Healing is about your developing and deepening your relationship with Love.

Divine miracles are natural occurrences. Love's angels are arranged for the specific purpose of setting up healing and carrying them through to completion. These angels are with you now and are operating for your best interest in every healing way. They are sending you messages at this moment, and every moment, night and day, whether or not you are listening. They are your guides for all your healings. Tune in. Learn from them. Listen. Grow.

Life is set up for you to win. The Love that created you wants you to succeed in every way. Consider yourself divinely authorized to do the work you came here to do. Know that Love causes you to be advantaged at all times. Love always makes available to you the principle of all healing.

Nothing is ever withheld for your healing. But it is up to you to seek out Love, apply Love's guidance, and to make it your devotion. There must be effort.

Not hard effort, but effort made that is consistent and full of love and gratitude, on a daily basis, and sometimes hourly or moment by moment. This is the practice of holiness.

You are not alone in holding the most precious spiritual thoughts in mind while the thoughts leave which antagonize and frighten you. When you have done your work fully, the fear will start to leave and inner peace will return. This is the way in spiritual healing.

Admit that healing is possible at this and every moment, always, and without exception. There is no such thing as "impossible to heal." There is no such thing as "too late for a healing." Take the attitude that all Love's healing possibilities – all of them – belong to you and now.

Give no power to the problem. As you continue to open to Love's infinite healing possibilities, continue also to release the entire problem. Release its feeling, fear, sensation, hurt, memory, imprint, others' opinions, and everything surrounding the problem, including its origin and history. Release it over and over and over, reminding yourself that Love is there in place of the problem. Love has been there all along.

Time cannot hold you in bondage. You are not waiting for the right time to be healed. Nothing in Love's glorious kingdom is delaying your healing. Your healing is available at this moment. Ask it to become visible. Honor it. Receive it. Do not outline how it will come. Just know it is here and is coming forward exactly as Love intends.

Question doubts about the healing. Re-program doubting thoughts that pour in. The following thoughts do not offer blessings of healing:

- "I may not be healed."
- "I am not healing."
- "I wonder if I will be healed?"

You are learning about Love in this instance and you will not be intimidated by doubting thoughts that harass the learning. Magnify Love, not doubt.

You are authorized to throw out all fear.

Fear does not serve healing. Through the power of Love, you can act to continually dismiss all fear. You are authorized to speak with authority and denounce fear.

Draw on the yang energies of archangel Michael and command the healing to come forward in the name of Love!

- "I command the appearance of lack, loss, and limitation to leave my finances so my innate abundance can be fully revealed to me!"
- "I command the feelings of loneliness, isolation, emptiness, and depression to leave my heart and to release me to Love's domain."
- "I command every symptom of illness and pain to leave my body. I am made whole from the top of my head to the soles of my feet. I receive this healing in Love's name and now."

Realize that whatever part – or parts – of your life that are living separate from Love must go. Humility is needed. Release pride and ego in doing healing work. This is a time to serve, learn, and surrender to Love. Through this humble approach, you are empowered with all healing. Your angels are on the case to support, enable, and bring forth full healing. It is the will of Love that you are blessed immeasurably in every way and now. All healing is available to you at this moment.

If there is something you must change about your attitude, your character, or your inner feelings, do it now. Ask Love for direction. Become aware. Stay with it.

Realize your placement of confidence. Either you are placing your confidence in fear and doom, or you are placing your confidence in trust and faith. Make the decision to place your confidence, as best you can, in Love's perfect outcome, which is blessing you at all times including now. Practice this confidence, knowing that Love is always with you.

Challenge discouraging beliefs

Discouraging beliefs are all about questioning the projected outcome, such as, "Is healing possible here, to me, and now?"

Beliefs are loaded with fear and false perception. Beliefs are never true, although they appear to be true and act as your own thoughts until they are addressed and challenged spiritually. Never, never believe a false belief.

Scott and I generally avoid sharing our problems with others, so that we do not expose ourselves to any discouraging or conflicting opinions. We take problems to Love and allow them to be worked out through prayer. If you are alone, however, it is helpful and wise to share with someone who is loving and spiritually-minded so you can receive comfort and healing support.

A false belief appears in thoughts such as:

- This healing may not be possible.
- This problem is incurable and impossible to heal.
- It's too hard.
- My prayers are not working.
- It will take a long time.
- Time is against me.
- I am limited in healing.

- I'm not sufficiently intelligent, experienced, wise, or spiritual to heal it.
- I'm at a disadvantage to be healed.
- I am not qualified to heal this.
- I never did have a talent for solving these types of things.
- I have a history of having this problem.
- I'm stuck and will most likely stay this way since I'm not equipped to change things.
- I'm not powerful enough to solve this.
- My parents told me many of these negative things about myself and convinced me.
- I'm overwhelmed by the problem.

Here are more of the common thoughts that prevent us from praying and meditating. They reinforce the belief that "healing is impossible or unlikely."

- I don't have enough time for daily spiritual practice.
- I have a hard time sitting still.
- Daily spiritual practice is boring. I don't like it.
- I can't organize myself.
- I feel bad that I don't pray or meditate regularly.
- I feel guilty because I know I should do healing work on the problem. I'd rather not think about it because I feel afraid.
- I don't understand spiritual healing work. It's too broad, too invisible, and I don't know what I'm doing.
- It's not that helpful.
- I mean to do it, but somehow I don't get around to it.
- Daily spiritual work probably won't be successful. It's no use.
- I am terrified that I won't be healed.

Remember, these beliefs are only thoughts! You

can choose any thought you want. You need to replace such thoughts that work against you. Replace them with solid, healing Love! How do you do this?

You listen to Love rather than these thoughts. You allow Love's healing thoughts to move in, while you set aside negative thoughts. As you continue to listen, you will find Love lifting you higher.

You may need to repeat this process of listening to Love and exchanging thoughts many times each day. This is what healing looks like. Do this until the healing is complete. It works.

You'll also find greater happiness than you ever dreamed of from doing this by the hour. Are true bliss, enlightenment, and ecstasy worth it? You bet!

Dig in with Love
& walk in the healing solution

"Enough already! It's time for this problem to be healed! I've prayed, meditated, and affirmed over and over again. What more can I do?"

Go forward in the face of what appears to be discouragement, frustration, and little healing progress.

Evaluate and build the case for healing even more. Double your determination, your resolve to heal, and your motivation, while reminding yourself that you have the patience, intelligence, ability, guidance, worthiness, and resources to be healed. Love is with you.

Listen more intently to Love's wisdom. Dig in your heels and learn something. Can you journal what you are learning? Then it is working!

Pull back and ask yourself, "What pattern is recycling? What is the belief up to? What am I really dealing with here?" Ask Love.

Listen to angel thoughts to show you the healing behind the healing.

Ask important questions that lead to your understanding, like, "What's the big picture here? What belief am I canceling? What am I healing in eternity right now?"

Realize that appearances are deceiving. Begin paying less attention to the appearance of the problem in your life and more attention to the divine solution unfolding to you.

Walk around in the solution, even if you don't know what it is.

Stop healing it "on the go." No more grabbing a quick affirmation and offering yourself a half-hearted prayer. Sit down and take the time to pray or meditate each day. Go into deep meditative stillness for longer periods. Listen to divine instruction from the same divine Source that is healing you and wants you healed.

Connect with this Source and stay connected. Healing is a holy experience with this Love Source. Give generous time to your holiness. Just because you think or worry about a problem doesn't mean you've given healing time to it. Focusing on the problem is not healing. Focusing on the divine solution and holding the space open for greater guidance and unfoldment is healing.

Adopt the healing attitude, "It's not my thought that says this is my problem." Disclaim ownership of the problem. It isn't yours. Stop buying into it. "This doesn't belong to me. I refuse to be held hostage by this any longer. I am taking a stand for this to be healed now and permanently."

Take a stronger stand to live outside fear in the arms of Love's healing presence. Ask more of yourself to feel this Presence with you more often throughout the day. Mentally check in and frequently.

Take a stronger stand to identify yourself and practice being Love's healing expression. Rather than thinking of yourself as a human with a problem, going through your day with the problem and feeling burdened and worried, change how you are identifying yourself and your sense of reality. Take the stand that you are the divine, living presence of Love. Be Love's icon of healing power today. Don't try to direct Love's energies. Just be the presence of Love and allow that to take care of everything else. Sit in your Love tower of power. Smile.

Take charge of the inner talk. Stop the inner talk that fears, hurries, rushes, feels behind, or wonders if you are going to be all right. Stop asking how the healing will occur and doubting whether it will occur. Let your inner talk come straight from divine Love's inner talk to Itself, "I am Love's presence. At this and every moment throughout eternity, I exist as perfect harmony, abundance, and total solution."

Remember, repetition is very important in healing. Beliefs, negative patterns, and old habits are so familiar to us that they are often hidden from us, buried deep within. Your spiritual healing practice of the repetition of prayer, affirmation, denial, and listening are vital for your healing awakening.

Persisting with repeated practice of right thinking – thinking in alignment with Love's reality – will cause you to triumph.

Be patient and you will see the enormous value of being educated in Love's Healing School.

Your willingness and determination to do all that is necessary for the healing – including daily treatments and consistently living the treatments – is winning.

Remember your healing attitude. Your "no nonsense" approach is authorized by Love. Know that your Love basis for healing is unstoppable.

Know that the problem is inferior and weak to Love's supreme power. The problem is unauthorized and will succumb to Love's prevailing presence as you persist. Your healing is normal and natural to Love.

Review the chapter "Tidal Wave Affirmations & Denials" to stay in the spirit of Love healing success. In fact, take time to review this entire book once again and look for the healing gems you may have missed as you were warming up as a spiritual healer. Take notes of special points to keep in mind as you move your life to a higher level of healing possibilities. Set new goals of what you are being led to think and do as a result of this healing teaching and your intuition. Let the angels influence and guide you.

How do you measure success in healing?

Let me show you what spiritual healing looks like from the inside out.

Here are some good ways to measure healing. You can ask yourself:

- What am I learning at this moment in eternity?
- What did I learn as a result of this painful/difficult experience?
- What did this experience teach me from Love's wisdom?
- Did I discover the divine reality about this situation? Can I identify it now?
- Will my learning be sufficient to stop recycling the belief I have suffered from?
- Did I cancel this belief from ever arising again?
- Am I listening to Love for these answers?
- Am I willing to grow and change?
- How have I learned to live in oneness with my Highest Self and purpose?

Sometimes our learning is the deepening of our faith or trust in Love. This was my experience when I worked on healing a lump in my breast. Here are some incorrect ways to measure healing.

- Did my spouse or life partner change and did we save the marriage?
- Is my body exactly the way I want it to be?
- Did I get a lot of money?
- Was I able to avoid going to the doctor?
- Did I find my true love mate?
- Did things work out like I planned?
- Did I get healed fast?

You learn in spiritual healing that Love often heals things in a surprising manner – in ways you couldn't have possibly planned or known. Such surprises occur especially when you think your case is simple, but you find out through healing that there is much more being healed, especially in your relationships, even with yourself.

You may have been in over your head, but not over Love's head!

Remember, your problem is not occurring because you are bad or being punished. Please never take the attitude of guilt. Generally, we suffer most from fear and ignorance. Do not think it is a negative experience to learn something that offers you greater knowledge and freedom – and also offers you healing.

Don't bully the healing work

Of course, your troubled heart deserves to receive full healing! Just don't allow yourself to cheapen the divine and holy experience of spiritual healing by pressing constantly for *your* expected outcome.

Don't be fooled by what you are really healing. You may not even know for awhile, but Love is revealing it and you will see. Your spiritual healings will be the richest experiences of your life.

Love's outcome is always right and good for you. Love's will is to bless you, not to punish you. Your ignorance is all you suffer from. Cancel the ignorance and you cancel the suffering. How? By listening to Love and growing.

Love will always provide the best possible solution for you. Your spiritual receptivity will help bring this forward. Healings often come in the most unexpected ways that you have not outlined or even considered. It's the divine and perfect way of re-arranging things to take you higher.

Protect your healing from pressures, stresses, judgment, and fatigue which come from fear and from always looking for the final outcome before you've done all the spiritual listening and following necessary for the healing.

Save yourself a lot of stress and don't harass the healing work by continually asking, "Where is my healing?"

There are times you will need to step back and evaluate your progress. When you do, do not attempt to answer this question by yourself. Ask Love for the answer. Never assume you are in charge of your healing. Love is.

Don't bully the healing work, saying, "If Love were really present, it would have healed me. I give up!"

Don't believe the superstition that if you suffer enough, you will have paid for the healing. Healing doesn't work that way.

Don't futurize your healing! Just do your full work staying in the present moment and let this take a natural course of spiritual action. Surrender to Love.

The big picture of life

The perception that we are in a time/space continuum having a human experience is deceiving. We're actually here to operate as divine beings and to use every obstacle in our lives to claim our divine origin and nature.

We do this by using divine principles of Truth and Love in order to learn about Love's true reality and free ourselves from all limitations. We listen for divine instruction. This is the only measurement of success in spiritual healing. You are proving your divinity. This is done, not by human perfectionism, trying to make everything perfect. It is done by the realization of your identity as divine and of the perfection that lies within you.

There are some lessons we are not going to get in any way other than going all the way into the fire and learning that the flame hurt only until we learned the wisdom of how not to be in the fire again.

As you persist repeatedly with healing prayer, and you continue to learn and grow from Love's messages, you will be led to make necessary changes in your thoughts, attitudes, habits, and actions. You will see results. This is the work of Love.

The goal is full realization of your divinity. This is also the beginning place of every healing. The irony of spiritual healing is that you start out where you want to wind up. Again, it doesn't seem logical, but it is the way of spiritual healing.

The realization of your divinity is your starting place as well as your finishing place in spiritual healing. The second irony of spiritual healing is that your divinity needs proving. By living your divinity more fully, you carry the power to ultimately heal everything.

Why? Learning something new about your divine Self is not enough. You must also walk it by putting what you learned into practice. This is the proof needed to neutralize beliefs.

Having your actions conform consistently with what you are learning about your true identity causes you to live outside the beliefs that most victimize you. What you learn needs to be put into action by you. This is how healing occurs.

Eternity lessons

Life doesn't make sense unless you understand that you are here on a learning curve. Everything you do and every relationship you have and every decision and evaluation you make needs to be from the standpoint, "What am I learning at this moment of eternity?"

Let every day be a moment-to-moment listening to divine Love. Always stay tuned in. Never stop asking Love for guidance about everything in your life. Let Love be your interpreter. See everything from the standpoint of eternity.

Big healings are the hardest won, yet they bring the biggest wisdom lessons of your life. They point the way, not only for a change for now, but for a permanent one for all eternity. Once you have truly learned a wisdom lesson, it is yours forever. Celebrate your learning!

Some people, who know little about true healing, may assume that when a spiritual healer refers to the need to learn a lesson, this implies condemnation or judgment of one who is sick or suffering.

Nothing, of course, could be further from the truth. Healing with Love means that we interact with Love and, in partnership with God, find our way through the fog of our life problems – with enormous compassion and gentleness for ourselves.

Just as when we learn to solve a problem in math and are then wiser, so it is in spiritual healing. Love is the teacher, helping us to solve life problems from a healing perspective. In some ways, you could say that spiritual healing with Love is like a course in humble listening to divine Love for answers. Healing empowers us.

When your healing depends on an eternity lesson, pay close attention. The problem may act as a distraction to the eternity lesson until you learn that what you are healing is more about learning the lesson than attaining an outcome. In the course of learning, however, your problem will also be healed.

Above all, stay with Love and don't get on a guilt trip. Do not allow a chronic problem to trigger guilt, shame, or a feeling of wrong. You are merely learning, and Love wants you to embrace yourself more than ever. Stay in Love's pure state and see your precious innocence.

Healing always involves humility. Humility, as we learn wisdom lessons, is not to be mistaken for being wrong. Humility means that we recognize that we have a problem, that we need help, and that we have the willingness to ask for help from divine Love. There is no judgment from Love just because we have a challenge. Let me ask you this. Who do you know that doesn't have a problem?

In spiritual healing, we do not view individuals as sinful or guilty. We see each person as Love's expression – divine, innocent, and completely good. This is what Love sees. This heals.

You are never pleading to Love for help. You are simply dipping into the great Niagara Falls of Love's healing messages that are pouring forth to you every moment. Let your healing process be wonderfully refreshing and powerfully healing. Love is with you.

You are on Love's journey. Let yourself be guided by Love for every healing. This is the Love you so deserve for all eternity!

Infinite blessings

Thank you for spending this healing time with me. I send you massive blessing and healing in all your prayers and endeavors to heal. My heart cares deeply that you are encouraged, that you live close to Love, that you are healed, and that you are blessed and a blessing to all others.

May you live and heal in Love forever.

About Shannon Peck

Shannon Peck is a full-time spiritual healer and teacher of healing as well as a past TV talk show host and prison chaplain.

She and her husband, Dr. Scott Peck, are Co-Founders of TheLoveCenter, a non-profit educational organization dedicated to holding the space for all humanity to live in healing Love. Together, they offer workshops on spiritual healing, love skills, relationships, and Love consciousness.

The Pecks co-author a popular monthly column as well as a free monthly email as part of *"A Course in Love & Healing"* that reaches people in over 30 countries. Shannon holds a Bachelors Degree in Religious Studies from Emerson Theological Institute.

**To contact Shannon Peck
for a healing appointment, call**

858-792-1779

To write Shannon Peck, send to

PO Box 830
Solana Beach, CA 92075

For lots of love & healing information, visit

www.TheLoveCenter.com

Notes

Notes

Notes

Notes